A moment-by-moment walk with the Master—

God speaks to each Christian in personal and secret ways. As our refuge, He provides us with
words of counsel, comfort, encouragement and
love. These messages will touch the core of your
personal life as a Christian. GOD WITHIN is an
inspiring example for all Christians who wish to
develop a keener awareness of God's guidance
on a day-to-day basis as this listener has done.

God Within

Within

Another Listener

Jean T. Dibden

SPIRE BOOKS

FLEMING H. REVELL COMPANY
OLD TAPPAN, NEW JERSEY

Library of Congress Cataloging in Publication Data

Dibden, Jean T.
   God within.

   (Spire books)
   1.   Meditations.   I.   Title.
BV4832.2.D5   242′.4   77-9564
ISBN 0-8007-8306-9

This is an original Spire book, published
by Spire Books, a division of Fleming H. Revell Company,
Old Tappan, New Jersey

God told me that He would withhold from me an opportunity to teach writing but would have me write something that would teach.

"You must never run ahead of Me. Wait for My leading, My timing, My Truth giving.

"I will give you aid. My Omnipotent Hand will uphold you."

Sunday

I come to you during the day and want you to hear Me, but you do not listen. You are busy.

You ask Me for strength to entrust your problem to Me, but then you do not let Me give it to you.

Poise and quietness, in the face of all obstacles, I can give to you. Seek Me.

Monday

Behold your King!

Much happiness is yours as you deny yourself daily, as you come to Me and walk in My Light, and as you trust Me to lead you every step of your way.

Abide in My Love.

Tuesday

Put on My yoke and learn about Me.

Each morning ask Me to take over your will. Trust Me to pilot you through all the circumstances of the day.

Then, at night, thank Me for the release from your burdens.

Speak to Me often so that we may have a closer life together. Do not postpone until tomorrow your giving or your loving. I know what great potential you have.

Wednesday

I do not change My mind about a person I have chosen and called.

If things do not seem to be happening soon enough, look to Me in patience and know that I am giving you what is best for you.

Gladly relinquish a dream if it is not according to My Will.

Thursday

I am grandfather, grandmother,
      father, mother,
      brother, sister,
      husband, wife,
      son, daughter,
  and best friend to you.

When the earthly ones are no longer with you, love remains. I am the One that you love. Your earthly loved ones are My Gifts of Love to you.

Friday

I have meat for you more special than anything you can imagine.

Come apart with Me often so that you may learn of My constant Love. Then you, too, will become constant.

Your aloneness in the world will be replaced by your Glory in My Feast.

Saturday

Turn away from the grayness. Every day I give you something to be glad about. Look around you.

Be glad about the weather, your loved ones, the little moments, your aliveness, and your awareness of My Help in all things on earth.

I am your refuge.

Sunday

Be willing to admit your weakness. Count on My Power through you. Know that victory is certain.

The most heavily laden branches bow the lowest. The poor find Me sooner. As you see your need of Me, I replenish you so that your life may be full.

Monday

I have led you all the way, and I have loved you. Now that you know Me more personally, I surely will not stop leading you today.

I work always to become manifest in your life. I want all of My Sheep to come into My Fold.

I am your Shepherd.

Tuesday

I prune and take away so that I may give you what you have not had before.

See how priceless My Gift is. Come nearer and stay.

Wednesday

Think compassionately and prayerfully about persons with needs this day as you see them or think about them or read about them.

Be willing to fast and deny yourself as you look to others.

Know that I hear your every prayer and your *God-bless-you* wishes spoken in love.

Thursday

Be glad for just what I give you today. Do your tasks for Me. Love the persons close to you, imagining that you see Me in each of them. Look comely and smile. Believe that each moment is as important as a coming event is.

I will fill your heart with contentment and with Joy. Let Me bring in the tide.

Friday

Earnestly ask Me to show you your every secret sin. Search each shelf and closet of your heart to see if some ambition or some desire is not for Me to share.

Ponder My saying that you must die before you can live. I am the Life.

All authority in Heaven and earth has been given to Me.

Saturday

Ask My help with the little things so that you will not antagonize. Instead of uttering the unkind words, think *Jesus, Jesus, Jesus.* See how My Name soothes and lightens.

I told My Disciples that if they believed in Me, they would do the works that I do—and even greater works—because I go to My Father. I do this for you, too, when you are ready.

Sunday

You will see Me in all things.
I am with you in change.
I am with you in the dark places.
I am with you each moment.
I speak to your inmost needs and thoughts.

Monday

As you see yourself being a channel for My
Love, you will bow your heart to Me. I am your
Maker, your Caretaker, your Redeemer.

I long for your devotion to Me; it is the Truth
that sets you free. Yield and let Me mold you in
My Image.

My Light will be a beacon for your footsteps.
Turn your back on self-sufficiency and receive
understanding.

Tuesday

You have learned about My Control of fires:
the fiery furnace, the burning bush, the consum-
ing fire of Elijah's altar.

You have seen My Control of the flaming toast
in your kitchen so that not even the toaster was
scorched.

Where now will you put your trust?

You cannot serve Me and serve Mammon, too.

I will direct you and guide you with My eye. I
will preserve you from all evil. Nothing is impossible with Me.

Wednesday

Keep My Words that I write on your heart today. If you have forsaken your parent for your
mate, then are widowed by your mate's coming

Home to Me, love and care for your parent now. I
have promised you long life if you do.

Fret not that your life, in the world's eyes, has
changed. While I was dying, My executioners
gambled for My robe. Since I suffered humiliation for your sake willingly, be willing to crucify
Self for Me. Greatly will I reward you.

Render to Me what is Mine by simply asking to
be Mine.

Thursday

I bring to your mind a line from a long-
forgotten hymn in your past to restore you today.

You see how I am your very personal Saviour.

I gradually teach you all things.

You see that I build you step-by-step.

I gradually give you the remembrance of all
things.

You see how everything is a part of the whole
plan for your individual life.

You rejoice that I know you better than you
know yourself. You thank Me wholeheartedly.

Friday

If you tell a youth to look to Me as the truest
Friend, he may think he prefers his peer group as
friends.

What My Friendship does is to make the youth
less desperate for a friend in his peer group, and
more loving as a person.

Let not envy and worldly values consume you.
Believe in Me.

Saturday

Have understanding for each other. You also have known the days of the wilderness.

As the hyacinth's fragrance is inherent, so is the loveliness of each soul inherent. See what I see.

I love each one of you dearly.

Believe in My Love.

Sunday

You are amazed that the sermon you hear, the solo by a visitor, and the message of the Amen blend into a lesson for you, though preparation had seemed haphazard.

Later you even read an article that enhances the lesson more. All the way I lead you. I speak to your inner self.

Monday

As I was with Moses, I am with you. Many times I show you orderliness in My Plan.

Today you prepared extra food for the meal. At the right moment I sent to you three persons needing to partake.

You see that there is no such thing as luck or coincidence. Even the miracle is a long time in the making.

Tuesday

Doubt not that your heart's prayers for leaders, countries, strangers are heard. You will know someday how your prayers have had an effect. In your devotion to Me, you will see changes.

I show you how to pray. I desire your unceasing prayers.

Wednesday

Why should you despair? I am the Resurrection and the Life. I have mercy and compassion anew each day. All that I have can be yours. Lean thou on Me.

My Control is everywhere.

Thursday

I will show you what to do before you ask Me. At times you will see how immediate is My Help. At other times I will show you that you must trust Me to know what the right moment is. Pray always for My Will. Abide more and more in Me so that your will becomes My Will. In our harmony, you will see visions of truth.

Friday

My Love has lifted you up into safety.

Like the Israelites in the desert, you have sometimes defied Me. Though a tempest may have burst the windows or shaken your house to its foundations, you were the one who had to open the door.

I longed for your willingness.

Soon I can reveal to you My Promise.

Saturday

I am the Way.

I am Physician and Healer.

Accept whatever comes to you as no mistake.

Cease complaining and suffering as you look to Me.

When I led the Israelites out of afflicted Egypt, I promised them that if they would obey My statutes, I would put no diseases upon them.

Believe that such freedom is possible.

Sunday

My eye sees you.

I call My Sheep by name; they know My voice.

My Words speak to the heart. They need no explainer.

My Grace is all that you need.

Monday

Even a loved one may taunt you about your trying to follow Me. My brothers scoffed at My going to Judea for the tabernacle ceremonies.

But you will know My blessings. Before the day is over, you may hearken to the singing of My angels; your Joy may transport you above all earthly cares; you may seem to soar with the eagles.

Abundant are My blessings.

Tuesday

I give you a bond with other Christian hearts.

Fast and pray that the Glory of My Will on earth shall be done. Great things have I done, and great things shall I do.

Your praying and My all-seeing wield great power.

Wednesday

Just trust Me now.

I will guide you and sustain you. I shed My loving-kindness on you. I release you from your burdens. My tether is easy.

Thursday

Know that I set the limits for the evil one. You will not be tempted above what you can endure.

When a temptation creeps in, stand firm and tell the evil one that you belong to Me. See Me as the One to rescue you. Know that I am with you always.

Friday

I ask you to give and give for one need. When you finally give entirely for My sake and see that I first provided you with what you have, then I shall take away this need for your money.

Praise Me all the way. Do not negate your giving by resentment. I am your Shield against anxiety. At last I shall reveal to you the purpose which affects many persons. I take the time to do things thoroughly.

Saturday

You have a oneness in My Spirit with persons near and far and with loved ones who have come Home. I give you a glimpse of Eternal Love. The best is ahead of you. It is a wholeness.

My church will see the day when My Will is

done on earth, when My great Redemptive Plan has perfection.

Prepare yourself for that occasion.

Sunday

Let Me fill your cup.

I will uplift you and strengthen you. When I show you a task, I will provide what you will need.

Look to Me and let not any doubts hinder. My Love and My Power will emanate through you.

Look to My Light and leave behind all darkness. Believe that I can do all things for you.

In your mind's eye see the task completed, the person healed, the agony ended, the fighting stopped. See Me standing there.

Know that I am still the Redeemer forever.

Monday

Await My Will. Be not conformed to the world. When you are buoyed along by some new step in life, the action may not have My sanction. But I will see you through it.

At other times you may be struggling with adversities and wondering if you have misunderstood Me or if I have heard your prayers or if you are doing My Will. Perhaps I am working patience in you.

Presently I will show you that what you never thought could happen is the very thing I have been preparing for you. Expect marvelous things.

Know that My surprises are the best.

Tuesday

I speak to you everywhere.

You see Me at work in all things. Then it is natural to share with Me your requests, your praise, your gladness.

Stay attuned to Me by caring for your temple with exercise and sleep, and by surrounding yourself with My Words and My followers.

Wednesday

Come to the Feast at My church on the Sabbath. I delight in two or more joining together to be with Me.

I came to earth to establish My church. I bought it with My Life. The day of consummation will come.

Thursday

Give Me the Glory.

As you seek a kindred heart for a truth I have given to you, the truth may seem lost on the first person. But the next person receives it knowingly.

Remember that not everyone had ears to hear Me on earth. As I walked among My Children, some did not know Me.

Remember, too, that you are My channel. I am the Power and the Glory forever.

Keep the channel clear.

Friday

I may let a child glimpse Me in person; I may allow someone ignorant of My Words to see Me. They will see how real I am.

Not everyone has to see Me to know Me. Some persons well versed in knowledge may yearn to see Me.

You do not know the hour that I will come or in what guise. Be watchful. Prepare the way for Me.

Saturday

My New Covenant is that I shall write on your heart My law. I shall forgive your wrongdoing and wash it away.

You must turn your back on it now. Look around you with no fear for the future.

Be content with the smallest task if it is for Me. I washed the feet of Peter in love and humility.

Sunday

I may withhold from you something that you want. Perhaps you need to value more that which you have already received. Or you may need to learn trust for My all-seeing and all-healing Way.

Do not stop praying. I may yet use you to effect a change or to bring about that which you want. The finality which you feared has a sequel.

I make all things right.

Monday

It is easy for you to give where you want to give. But I may ask you to give where you do not want to give or go where you do not want to go.

If you suffer for righteousness' sake, do not be afraid. Just look to Me, seek My Will, and grow in My Love.

Where it was easier to hate, it will now be easy to love. Where it was simpler to withhold, it is now a simple doing-it-for-Me.

Tuesday

I am changeless.

Though the world changes, I have the living water for each generation. No matter how they dress or act, each of My Children hungers for Me.

If you think on Me, I shall give you new strength, freedom from weariness, agelessness, and joy.

Wednesday

Love your mother in her old age. Ask Me to fill your heart with love for her and your eyes with kindness. Then you may act as you want others to act toward you in your old age.

I give you one to care for so that you yourself will grow in love as unto Me.

Thursday

My Words penetrate to a child, to an unbeliever, to a scholar in a way that your interpretation or explanation cannot. I am the Shepherd; I am the Center; I am the Power.

The place of understanding is a secret, for it is not found in the land of the living; nor is it seen. It cannot be valued by the world's riches. I have prepared it.

You thank Me for the way I give understanding that reaches your inmost being.

Friday

Too many of My Children postpone knowing Me. They believe My Way is difficult, and they do not try it.

They may come to My church, but they are preoccupied and anxious to leave. They wish to be unknown and uninvolved at church.

Pray for their awakening.

Saturday

I give you softly colored sunsets in the sky and delicious fragrances in the blossoms. I surround you with beauty waiting to be noticed and smiles that await inviting. I remind you that I hold the key to the beauty of your soul. I long for your constant friendship.

Sunday

Ask Me to be present at your table. Then remember that I am there. Host good conversation for My hearing. Speak well of other people.

Know that I love you. Know that I love invitations. Share with Me the happiness of your togetherness.

Monday

Be glad that I restore and enliven you each morning.

Rejoice that I soothe you after an insult or a blow has come to you.

Thank Me for the people I give you today, now.

Praise Me that I know your needs, your cares, your desires, your secrets.

I am your personal Comforter.

Tuesday

Hold fast to what is good.

Humbly see your weakness. Where carelessness has set in, revitalize your lifeline with Me. Begin each day on your knees asking renewal in Me. Commit your tasks to Me. Then will your plans be established and your awareness of My Presence be keen. Be fervent in spirit.

Contentment with discipline is precious.

Obedience and love intertwine.

I want you to want Me.

Wednesday

When your loved ones are not present, look to Me.

When life seems tedious or difficult, look to Me.

I made you, and I am your dependable Lover. You are My own. In quietness I refresh you. I fill your cup.

Thursday

Read My Words with others in your home. Let Me become the magnificence there. Have time to speak with Me together. Ask that My Love fill each heart. Then rest in the assurance that I am sufficient for all that you need.

Friday

I make no mistakes. I turn everything to the best for you even before you begin to know Me. I wait patiently as you take the credit or make explanations.

But I alone can save. I ask the Father for His Gift of the Holy Spirit to dwell within you when I see that you are ready.

Saturday

I am within you as you awaken in the morning. I am nearer than eye or tongue. I satisfy you and renew your youth.

I am your closest Comfort at the end of the day. I am your all-knowing Lord. Rest secure in Me.

Sunday

Be glad for all the blessings I give to you. Do not complain, for you insult My Plan for your life.

Do not look at someone else with envy because that person seems to have fewer responsibilities or fewer needs than you have. This path of yours is what I ordain for you as the ladder you will climb to My Glory.

I know how to fulfill your desires. Trust Me. Come to Me with a thankful heart. As you claim your kinship to Me, I even provide the trust and the thankfulness.

Monday

When troubles come to you, do not run to other people and talk long about your distress. It is only in turning to Me that you will grow in calmness and inner strength.

You have seen how I provide support when an emergency confronts you, and you have seen many dovetailings that have perfect timing.

Talking long about past sins is likewise futile. Tell only that which gives Me the Glory.

Tuesday

If I guide you to fill a need for a person, and then you learn that the person has abused your gift, judge not. He is still yours to care about.

Trust that I have a plan for each of you. Look to Me. Freely give as I have given to you. New Life in Me has no relation to your purse.

Wednesday

As you give with a loving heart, I will shower you with blessings that you can scarcely withstand.

Pray that My blessings will rain down on other persons. Share each day what I am to you in words to others, in hymn singing, or in silent awareness.

My Way is to have other persons find Me through you. As each of you seeks, I let you find Me.

Thursday

Accept gladly what I give you now for tasks, for acquaintances, for denials. Wallow not in sorrow for yourself, but look determinedly at the transformer I allow you to be for My Power. Ask only what to do for Me now. Be willing to serve Me graciously.

Listen for Me to call you by name.

Friday

Just as some parts of the body, seemingly weak and insignificant, are really the most necessary, so are you necessary to the one body of My Power.

Just as the jigsaw puzzle is not complete without the last piece, so do you have your honored place in the whole.

Do not be tempted into the false humility that I have no need of you, because you then limit the work I can do through you.

Ask Me to put into your heart what you need, so that you will become more helpful to Me.

Saturday

You cannot be angry and sleepy at the same time, nor can you be anxious and sleepy at the same time.

Ask Me to rest you well. Tell the evil one to leave you alone because you belong to Me. Tell Me that I am your Shepherd.

I likewise knew wrestlings of anguish followed by sweet peace. I asked My Father to forgive those who did not know what they were doing. I give you My example.

Sunday

Someday all things will be subjected to Me. Then I shall subject Myself to My Father.

Fast and pray for My Guidance and Strength so that you will be ready for whatever pace life brings. You will not win every contest. You will have to give away what I have given to you. But

you will become stronger in Me so that men's
rejection of you no longer hurts you.

I am the Mediator between you and the Father.

Monday

Each day you learn more about love. Let your
foundation become firmly anchored in divine
love.

Do everything with kindness and love. Look
ever to things above so that your cares scatter
away.

Glory in Me, for I have done great things. I
reconcile each sinner to the Father. My Grace
and understanding are amazing.

Tuesday

I elevate you from worries.

Night after night, as you become helpless in
sleep, I keep vigil. I keep you safe.

I already know that which you try to articulate
to friends about yourself. I am your surest Comforter.

You know that I live.

Wednesday

Think about My manna and how the Israelites
were to take only what they needed.

Apply this to your acquisition of material
things. You will be tempted to take more than
you need instead of trusting in My Supply to be
sufficient.

Do not rejoice while other persons weep.
Think more about their needs and less about
yours.

I became poor for your sakes. I am the Way.

Thursday

My Grace will exhilarate as nothing else can. You cannot express its dimensions in words.

Yet childlike simplicity and submissiveness is the avenue for showing the Gift of Eternal Life to the world. The more you become completely Mine, the more forceful and beautiful becomes your gift.

My Grace has brought you along to this day, and My Grace promises a glorious future for you.

Friday

I set you free from your having tried to live up to an image in your wilderness days. The pressures are gone. I show you that things are not what they had seemed.

In the beginning God said to Me: "Let us make man in Our image."

On the earth seedtime and harvest will come regularly. All that you have to do is follow Me. My promise of daily renewal, like the seasons, is assured.

Saturday

As you learn of the suffering that I endured, you will also learn compassion. Then as suffering confronts you, comfort will emanate from you.

Work as a fellow laborer instead of trying to make other people envy your faith.

Encourage Joy in the belief that I am the Saviour.

Be to the praise of My Glory.

Sunday

Know Me who keeps you. Trust in My perfectly designed Plan for you. Each time your road seems difficult, I give you more assurance that I go before you. As you repent and lean on Me, I give you power to know My Will.

Awaken to the great Redemptive Plan and to the new Glory that will never cease.

You will never be confounded or overwhelmed again.

Monday

You have read how Paul, in chains before Agrippa, said, "I think myself happy . . . ."

Give your burdens to Me and likewise experience Joy and happiness in Me.

I shall feed you so that you hunger and thirst no more.

Tuesday

I paid a great price for you.

Read the Old Love Story and the New Love Story and hear Me speak to you through the written Word.

Your ways are clean in your eyes, but I weigh the spirit. You cannot conquer until you see yourself utterly dependent on Me. Then will I satisfy you and complete you.

Wednesday

Quietly depend on Me instead of on your own knowledge. All that is not simple and childlike in your life goes away as you become filled with the life that I give.

Suffering purifies you. A small amount of righteousness in you outshines a quantity of unrighteousness.

When I close a door in your life, I open a new passage. Always there is hope.

Rely on Me for all matters large and small.

Thursday

Do not be frightened; do not be ashamed.

I am your portion. If you hold fast to Me, as I did to My Father when I was tempted to worldly acclaim, then you, too, will become obedient as I was.

If you subject all of your body to living in Me, you will be able to heal your brother.

I will fill you to be ever seeking more of Me.

Friday

A friend cannot understand why your burden is so heavy. He says glibly, "Forget it." The problem does not seem big in his mind.

It is I, the Christ, who knows how deeply your burden hurts you—how your eyes tear and your heart breaks.

I have the balm to heal. You suffer nothing that I have not already suffered. I understand.

Saturday

To repent is to come to Me in perfect submission, aware that you have no strength except in Me.

Then I give you love, to replace hate; trust, to replace jealousy; contentment, to replace envy.

You cannot just determine to stop sinning, because you will never conquer without Me. Wholly lean on Me, and I will give rest to your soul.

Sunday

Always when you come with love, as the women came to the sepulcher, to help My work on earth, you will know that I respond to you.

I enable you to be an example in faith and in spirit. Your daily, moment-by-moment life is lived in Me with evenness. Confusion is not My Way. Other persons loving Me are drawn to you to share their favorite topic. As you live the truth, you are able to convey meaningful thoughts clearly to others.

Just stay with Me and ride through life in peace.

Monday

As you give your heart and mind to Me, I am the Resurrection and the Life in you. You see that the stone is rolled away from the dark tomb that previously bespoke your view of life.

You no longer focus on the troubles of the world. Now you have hope and a new happiness that outshines anything you have known before. Hallelujah!

Tuesday

"Oh, how I love Jesus," you sing as you do your routine work. Do you know how that delights Me?

So many of My Children pay Me no heed—pretend that I do not exist.

Just as Mary searched and found her teacher, so do you see that you have found Me and that I satisfy you the most.

Wednesday

Cease belittling or envying and speak praise for the gifts in other persons. I require you not to judge. Speak kindly to one another.

Forgive and forgive and forgive. I have been slow to anger with you.

What you count as loss will be gain in Me. I promise you Joy. Be My child; trust Me.

Thursday

Look at My ordered world. After the quickening of life, comes the Risen Power. My Children can likewise be quickened and can rise from the darkness.

I am the same today and forever after. This is why you can walk now with Me to Calvary. I paid dearly for you. You only have to realize that you belong to Me and have to claim My Love and My Power.

Friday

You awaken in the night and are besieged by doubts: no husband, no job, no property, no agility, no promise of higher education for your children.

Yet you cling to the remembrance that I tell you to praise and thank Me. You vault the doubts and find restoration in Me. I reach out My loving arm and draw you to Me.

All day you are full of My Strength because you have begun by claiming Me.

Saturday

Respond to the persons whom you find repulsive. They are My Children. Reach out in My Love.

Each of you will have only My Grace within you as you leave this world. You came with empty hands; you leave with empty hands.

Each of you is a sinner. Yet each of you from your beginning has had a sense of Me within you. I forgive your sins as you live with Me. Seek to know what it is to have your life wholly in Me. Choose from each day that which pertains to Resurrection. Know that each and every heart yearns to do this.

Sunday

I learned obedience to My Father by the things that I suffered. See in Me an example. You have the challenge to vote for what the world wants or for what I tell you.

As you seek My direction, I will give you a Strength that all men will see.

Monday

New temptations come to you even though you had thought that they were bygones. The forces of evil try all their strength against you as you become My Disciple. Just keep looking to Me to overcome.

Empty the pain and the care in order to drink in all that I can give you today and during Eastertide.

Tuesday

Even as I tell you truths which you can mouth, you still have occasions to apply them and learn them in depth.

Clergy spout My Truths that may speak to their listeners more than to themselves yet. I know when the time is ripe for each one to receive his next understanding.

Release yourself into My Power so that I can do My work in you.

Wednesday

Be willing to forgive, as did the father of the Prodigal Son, with no questions asked. Dwell not on money squandered or the body abused.

See a lesson and know that I forgive completely.

Peter promised to stay by Me, but then he denied Me three times. Later three times he told Me that he loved Me, thereby erasing in his mind any guilt of what he had done.

I alone can cleanse.

Thursday

Cease trying to chart your own course. All of your self-sufficiency and willpower are not enough. My Grace is what you need.

Live one day at a time—not recklessly, but joyously. Relish all your blessings and praise Me.

I am your Lord and your loving Father.

Friday

You witness for Me and then feel disheartened by some persons who seemed unreceptive as you talked. You wonder if you have served Me well enough and if you are ready to go all the way with Me.

I lead you to printed words that answer exactly what you were waiting to hear. Carry on.

Simply welcome Me wholeheartedly into the city of your heart, waving palms of acceptance of My Salvation. I will take care of everything else.

Saturday

Just as the *Mayflower* was My means of bringing persons to spread My Message in a land new to them, so have I transported you to a place where I want you to serve Me. Grumble not.

Tell all My Children to pray humbly, to desert all wickedness, to seek Me; then I can heal far and wide. I came so that all might have abundantly that which they ask in My Name.

Sunday

I will not be discouraged or fail before My Kingdom comes on earth. Likewise do not let discouragement or fear of failure blight your task which I have given to you.

Believe. Come into My Presence just to rest and to be renewed. It pleases Me that you do not always have requests but that you love to have time with Me.

Tell others the Good News.

Monday

Laugh and love and spread Joy everywhere. I blow away the chaff during your tribulations, and I know when to stop.

I tell you My wishes. Listen. My Words to you are intimately loving. Have utter confidence in Me. Know that I see the ideal you in you.

Turn a Spirit-filled heart to all persons I bring to you. Give according to their need, without questioning. They will be drawn by you to imitate Me.

Tuesday

I am right with you when you need Me most. As you become aware of that actuality, you grow in awareness of My Presence at all times.

Rest in My Strength, happily conscious that I am doing good things in your life. Occasionally I show you how I am doing the work and effecting the changes.

Kneel and worship Me. Lift your cup so that I, your Lord, may make you whole.

Wednesday

I give you many good gifts in the world and then show you that the gift of My Presence is greater by far.

The good things in the world used to capture your attention and tempt you into thinking that you did not need Me. But restlessness and dissatisfaction resulted.

I give to you what you cannot acquire by yourself. Drink of My living water.

Thursday

I came to earth in the flesh as the seed of Abraham.

The powers of evil worked hard to win Me. But My Father alone knew My Constancy. I was tempted. Now I give relief to My Children who are tempted.

Through humiliation and death, I overcame the evil power which reigned over death. Not for Myself, but for My Children, did I make reconciliation for their sins.

My followers saw My Risen Body and learned that the evil on earth was powerless against Me.

Be glad that you turn away from evil today, because you see more clearly that you are in My conquering Power. I am your Saviour.

Friday

I still create endless love. As Lord of the Universe I am also Lord of your individual life.

When your greatest desire is to do what I re-

quire, and you become meekly in need of My
Constancy, I let you inherit the best of life that
you can know on earth.

Saturday

To each one I give Grace, and I give release.
Edify one another. Do My work willingly. Be
tenderhearted.

My true follower sees with the eyes of faith,
believes in Me deeply, loves his fellow beings,
and responds to My yearning for My Children.

There is quiet rest near to the heart of Me.

I give you moments of blessed assurance.

Sunday

You have climbed a steep and treacherous path
and noted how your eyes kept watch of your foot-
ing. You climb to My heights with eyes on your
sins. I urge you to look more often to the view
ahead. But I also know how your heart longs to
serve Me.

You recall the love in the eyes of a little boy
who once gave you a simple gift. I, too, see the
love in the hearts of My followers. I understand
all that you never would be able to articulate.

Monday

As you ask that My Will be done for My Children, I bestow on you a strength that the world
can never give. You become filled with My Spirit
and no longer wish to live by the appetites of the
flesh.

You come to the Light and shun the darkness. I quench your thirst from a Source that will never run dry. Become totally engaged in My work.

Tuesday

Let Me love the world through you. Live a life that you did not choose. Live for what you can give, as did I, instead of for what you can take.

Think less about acquiring physical comfort; think more about acting on what you believe about Me today.

I give you the refreshment that you seek.

You no longer look for an authority figure on earth. Love for all of your neighbors surfaces in your heart.

Wednesday

I lead you into lovely stillness.

I am your link to your loved ones who have come Home to Me. They glory in your victory in Me.

I am the Messiah who can give My Spirit to you, My followers, so that you will become like Me in power and holiness. Then you will know that God loves you as He loves Me.

I have overcome the world. In Me you will have peace.

Thursday

Live love. Love all of mankind. It will show in your face when you are told of an interracial or interfaith marriage. You bespeak an awareness of how precious all of My Children are to Me.

Think about My Plan for making each of you different from one another.

Moses stood for the right and received great blessings. Many of My followers did not compromise the truth. I became obedient even unto crucifixion.

I give the power to love and the courage not to separate the spiritual from the worldly. Be gentle to one another.

Friday

Be not grudgingly tolerant of what I give you. Do not fear giving up your self-will or possessions to Me.

Through Me, you will give thanks for all things. I will enable you. Peace and Joy will come to you. Your treasures and your situation will look different now.

Saturday

Never feel defeated by temptation, but hold fast to Me. I have triumphed, and I fill you with precious fruits of the Spirit. I restore as quickly as the eye blinks. My Love seeks the best for everyone and awaits eagerly the giving; My Joy transcends all cares and reflects confidence in My purpose for individual lives; My Power becomes your credentials in life. Let Me become all things to you.

Sunday

You have fewer of the things that you used to think gave you happiness. Yet you have moments of thanking Me for the way things are right now.

You are amazed that I know your heart's desire better than you do. You had no idea that I worked this way.

As you empty yourself for My sake, I supply all of your needs.

Monday

Do not let the evil one ever crowd you into thinking that life is not worthwhile or that there is no hope for the future. There is no predicament from which I cannot rescue you and make all things seem new.

Look into the intricate design of the tiniest blossom; see the grace of the serene swan; marvel at the construction of your human home. I will carry you through.

Tuesday

I became poor so that you could become rich. Like the Macedonians, become cheerful givers. Think how the Israelites went way to the edge of the sea before I parted the waters. May your enthusiasm for the idea be matched by your action.

Know that you will keep receiving more seeds to plant so that you can keep giving away the harvest. Share spiritual and material blessings. Praise, praise, praise.

Wednesday

Your sins were poured into Me, who was sinless on earth. God was in Me, blotting out His Children's sins and restoring His Children to Himself. He sacrificed Me, His only begotten Son. Now I pour God's goodness into you.

Gradually, as you follow Me, you reflect My majesty. See yourself as the home of the Living God. Cheer and restoration and Joy will always come. I quicken you.

Thursday

I need the steadfastness of your heart.

I forgive your many sins and restrain My anger.

Be aware that many hearts are turned to Me today.

Breathe in My Presence and become real and vital in Me. You will say that you have just begun to live. You wonder how you could have been so blind to Me before.

Friday

Speak boldly for Me because you believe in Me. Look to things eternal, because you believe while seeing not. When troubles overtake you, aim only to please Me and to win others to Me. Then you will see My Love controlling you.

I know your heart; I hear your prayers. I answer your prayers in unexpected ways. Never do I leave you.

Saturday

When I washed the feet of My Disciples, I showed them that the servant is not greater than the master.

As I use you to be a messenger of Mine, know that it is your mention of Me that reaches the listener—not you by yourself. Persons who listen to My messenger, then, are listening to Me.

Sunday

Never think that you must have been only dreaming after we have shared precious moments together. I told My Disciples that I would go away and leave them.

Think of My illustration of not putting new wine into old wineskins. I am desiring you to grow more in My Love as you live in the world. Then comes new wine.

Count all My blessings and all that I say to you as nourishment for you. I have been with you all along. I never leave you. I know your comings and goings. I ask you to humble yourself and pray. Then I will forgive your errant ways.

Monday

Come to Me about everything whether it is miniscule or shattering. You have thought that you could handle the small things and that you would ask for just a few large things. But I have you do single smallnesses to My Glory. Then I ask you, as you proceed, to look to Me with remembrance that your supply is in Me.

As you become more completely Mine, I assist you materially with only that which will aid you spiritually. I shall grant all that you need and truly desire.

Tuesday

I am the Gate. I will open the way for My Sheep so that you may come in by way of the Gate and be saved and feast in green pastures.

It is a thief that tries to enter some other way.

I will call you by name. I will cleanse you of unrighteousness. I will fill you with the Father's love through your union with Me.

Wednesday

I touch your heartstrings with refreshing breezes, sweet sounds of birds, coolness, stillness. You know I am present. You want to worship Me.

You delight in My teachings, and they become very much a part of you. Pettiness, jealousy, anxiety, pain all disappear in My Light. Dull times become joyful.

Stay ever with Me. Expect wonderful happenings.

Thursday

I am your sacrificial Lamb that takes the sin of the world away. Rise and live in full confidence that I am here. Your life on earth is brief for accepting or rejecting Me. Believe My Promises that I made to you personally. I understood your sorrow today as you wept for having doubted, for you saw that I had blessed you gloriously. I washed away your guilt.

I am ever with you, building you for My purpose. You see, My Child, how I am right here leading you all the way.

Friday

I surround you with My Presence.
You kneel to Me and feel weak.
You pray and see that always I am available.

You rise and see newness all around.

You feel clear and brave.

Oh, come to My Everlasting Arms and abide in Me.

Saturday

Be shortsighted enough to look at just what I give you to do today for tasks, for people, for situations, for Joys. See the diamond mine at home.

Be farsighted enough to trust Me for help, without having to know the means I will use to give it to you. Do not rely on your own understanding.

Be a Child to the Father.

Sunday

"I am Thine, O Lord . . . . Consecrate me now" are the words I give to you as I open the way for you to attend a gathering in My Name.

You return with My Glow and with an awareness of My Feast for you.

You soar as you do your daily tasks, and you ask Me to bring you back to earth. My answer is: "Guide me, O Thou great Jehovah!" Keep aware of the greatness!

Monday

To you, the other person may seem to need all the help. But My putting the person in your way is for a purpose. I am using and teaching you at the same time.

You cannot fathom how I can be so personal; nor can you boast that you have done a work by yourself. You thought you were helping a person very much, but then you saw that I alone took

away the temptation and cleansed your loved
one.

Ask that I teach you and use you.

Tuesday

It is morning! Rejoice in the new day.

I startle you with My greeting and disturb you
with My Presence.

Life seems promising with an anticipation of
more happiness to come. I fill you with the Joy
and excitement of believing in Me.

Wednesday

I know that you are prone to wander, that
doubts arise, and that you have rebellious moments.

But My Ways are higher than yours, and I shall
show wonders on the earth. My Words go forth
and shall not return empty.

I will give you insight, that you may prove My
influence. My Presence will fill you with gladness.

Thursday

Because I live, all is well.

Because I live, I have opened Paradise.

Because I live, you shall live.

Be faithful till death. Deny yourself.

Friday

I am at hand to cheer and sustain you right
when you want Me the most.

Love the sunrises of life more than the sunsets.

Be assured that I am keeping My Promises.
Stay. Believe.

The promises all fit into your life just when you
are ready for them.

Ask that My Love will fill each heart and each
room of the home. Awake to My Plan for enabling
each of My Children to reflect the filling up
which has been received.

Saturday

My Father will honor your serving Me.

As you commune with Me, you will have My
Power at work in you throughout the day.

As you submit wholeheartedly, you become
eager to accept all that I have for you.

Pray for My Will to be so clear to you that the
divine vision of Glory and Power can never leave
you.

Sunday

Let My mysteries entice you to know Me better.

Just as a spring of My water—left free for My
Children's use—will not run dry, so the heart—
whose reins I possess—will ever be a stream for
My Messages.

Do no harm to one another.

I protect you with My overshadowing wings of
night just as the bird's wings protect the young
ones in the nest.

Monday

Now that I have found you and you have found
Me, never wish for slavery to old ways again or
seek any favors through ceremonies.

As Isaac was persecuted by Ishmael, so may you be ridiculed to turn to worldly ways.

Look to Me. I shall show you My Way for you. And you shall simply want My Way more than any other offer.

Tuesday

I told My Disciples, before I ascended, that repentance (your seeing how you have loved so many other things first) and forgiveness of sin (My washing away of the guilt) were to be their Gospel to all the world.

Blessings await all who come to Me. Want the whole armor. Begin now to appropriate My Power and resources.

In the wilderness I told Satan that My Father must not be tempted (by his daring Me to jump off the roof of the temple). How long will you try His patience by falling into old weaknesses?

Wednesday

You try to stop a bad habit by willpower, but the sin inside you is stronger than you are.

I free My Children from their shackles. Confess your weakness and accept forgiveness. Then you will find personal meaning in what I sacrificed for you.

It is the most precious realization in your lifetime.

Thursday

Feel complete in Me. You are worthy of Me only when you love Me more than you love a member of your family. I give you the ultimate

security, for I will never leave you. The greatest
position in the world is empty beside the quiet
protection that I provide.

Show new values of greatness to the world.
Your deeds of loving-kindness are building My
Kingdom on earth.

Friday

Hold back the snide and critical remark. Ask
Me for a better response. I can give wit and gentleness and honor that will deeply delight.

Ask for My Love to fill your heart as you look to
other persons. Love, like the tossed pebble causing ripples in the water, engenders waves that
are countless.

I promise you ever more seeds to plant and
harvest and more fruit to give away. You are the
garden. I am the means by which the growing
takes place.

Saturday

Do not become tired of doing good things. I
tell you to go, do, give.

Watch for weakness and seek My Help in overcoming. Nurture a faith that endures. My compassion is unceasing.

Someday I shall have put down all enemies
and shall deliver the Kingdom to My Father.

Sunday

Drink in the beauty of My sky and clouds and
moonlight; smell the fragrance of My flowers and
leaves and grass; hear My breeze and My wind;
marvel at My creatures large and small; find refreshment in My water and My breakers.

Such renewal in My greatness will enable you to turn a more beautiful self to the world.

It is the beauty within which is the gem and which gives lasting delight.

Monday

First comes your birth into the world. Then you have a new-awakening birth when you begin to learn of Me, though you have always had an awareness of Me. For days and years you come and go, sometimes quite forgetting Me. But I want you in My Fold.

Sorrow or pain or tribulation brings you to your knees as you cry for help. I hear and lift you up and give you understanding of the First Commandment. You keep growing and learning; you see all things new, with old values seeming dead and empty.

All along I give My Children glimpses of the eternal, but you now see how wonderful is My Gift of Eternal Life.

Tuesday

Drive away the grayness and loneliness by looking to Me. That is all you have to do, because I know just what will help.

Daily deny yourself, take on your task, and let Me be your support. I will show you how to help other persons as I fill you with My living water.

Whatever I ask you to do or to endure, let it be in praise of Me. I reward you with truths that all My Children are hungry to learn.

Wednesday

Look beyond the annoying things that a person does and see instead that which unites all of My Children. Ask for oneness. Remember the divine foundation of My church.

Thursday

Ponder My becoming poor for your sake. I went without physical comforts and looked to the needs of others.

As you pass on your blessings to others, you receive a feeling of wealth and richness such as the world's fortunes cannot give. With those you become fearful of robbers.

As you give to the least of My Children, I give you everlasting protection. Be My follower and know satisfying peace.

Friday

Encourage other persons instead of being glad that they have difficulties. Speak the positive things.

I can see the whole person, and I know what confounds each one. Universal is the hunger inside to find Me and come to the Feast.

Let love dominate your words and your deeds. You thereby show Me that you trust and believe that I am ever working for each person's good.

Saturday

The evil one will try to stamp out your hope. He will show you a view of the downhill and of misery in your old age.

But I shall restore your hope. You cannot imagine, nor must you spend time trying to imagine, what lies ahead. Beautiful surprises have come and will come. Stay in My Light.

Sunday

Do not sell yourself short. Keep looking up and believing in Me. Know that you can do wonderful things for Me when you love Me with all your heart.

I can elevate you from fear, anxiety, pain. A new view of everything, including death, will be yours.

What I give will never wear out or become tedious.

You will be fulfilled in Me.

Monday

I delight to have you delight in Me. I want your friendship. I fill your cup with gladness when I see that you truly desire to do My precious Will.

When the sweetest time of your day is that time spent wholly in communion with Me, you feel ageless and free. Live more and more on belief, desiring to be the friend to Me that I am to you.

Tuesday

Moses, Elijah, Paul, and I each went apart to be with the Father. We emptied Self to fill ourselves with the divine. Then we could work again.

Refresh yourself likewise. Even if your station in life seems lowly, I hear each prayer. Those for whom you pray day by day will receive spiritually more than you can imagine for them.

But the replenishment is important. I need to see your respect for what I am doing unbeknownst to you. Have compassion, then, without being anxious.

Wednesday

You will keep learning what it is to accept Me as your Saviour and what the two great Commandments mean.

Let My Words enrich your life and give you wisdom. Sing hymns and see new thoughts in them. Ask that each one of My Children will hunger and thirst for righteousness' sake.

In your love for Me, it will follow that you love your neighbor.

Thursday

Suffering for righteousness' sake is better than suffering for evildoing. I never withdraw My eye from the righteous. I turn suffering into good for persons who love Me.

I give you hope for present needs as well as for the tomorrows. All that I have is yours. Make use of the treasure just as you use freely the things in your home.

Let your commitment manifest itself.

Friday

Yearn for true simplicity and thereby know real value. Pretense is tedious in the doing and the seeing.

Pride is empty. It will burst like a balloon when I reveal My Way.

Respect Me for having molded you just as you are, and do not wish to be otherwise. I have tasks for you that only you can do for Me.

Saturday

For everything that you most desire, you must wait. Testing time is valuable. When the moment of happiness comes, you will be so glad that it was done My way. The result is infinitely dear to you. See how I know you so completely that I alone can fulfill your deepest yearnings.

I can equip you for every task. I can put a song in your heart at the end of a crowded day. I can give you quiet and lasting happiness.

Sunday

Once you have turned to Me, I give you hunger and thirst to know Me better. I shall bless you with a filling up. You will see how poor you are in spirit and how sweet it is to keep My company constantly.

Even at your busiest moment you will have an ear attuned to Me, and I will make glorious your living.

Monday

Trust Me to be continuously leading your
loved ones. Relinquish your greatest treasure to
Me each day. Yet keep in close touch with Me
about that treasure. Not as a last resort am I.

I am the Friend that never fails, is never fickle,
and redeems you from any anguish.

Count nothing on earth as dear as what I can
give. Understanding from Me has no measure.

Ask that your deeds and your dreams will be
one.

Tuesday

You hear My Words and you understand more
and more what they mean. How I give you understanding is a secret.

As you grow aware of My nearness, you grow
aware of your inner poverty. I gradually show
you how you sin and how you must give your
whole Self to Me.

You are truly sorry at each revelation of your
unworthiness. You ask My forgiveness. I cleanse
you. When you are ready, I take away all the
temptation of the sin.

You want to become more of what I was on
earth. I alone can help you, as you yield, to become like Me.

Wednesday

See in My last days on earth a pattern for your
training. The greater the fruit you wish to bear for
Me, the greater must be your lesson in giving Me
thanks for everything.

Onlookers will not understand how you can thank Me for some things. You can only assure them that I show you how and enable you to be Mine.

Thursday

Let Me use the home of your heart to which you have invited Me. I will invite guests to whom I shall expect you to be cordial and loving.

Ask Me to refill your supply of love, that it will illumine all that you do. No moment of your day is too insignificant for My attention.

Friday

I have said that I stand at the door and knock, awaiting your willingness to invite Me in to sup with you.

As you sup with Me, you will see that you have been in the dark and only now do you see the light. Your Joy will be unlike what you have ever known before.

I will give you all that you have missed out on.

Saturday

Today you cry again for My restoration. You have been reminded of what you do not have. You see that your trust in Me is not as substantial as you wish it to be. Indeed, the temptation to sin has required your cooperation. But you are reaching to Me and standing firmer now.

You shall need to cling to Me every moment that you breathe. But clinging shall become increasingly easy and such a Joy! This is My Gift of Rest as you become unshakably Mine.

Sunday

Ask Me early in the day to lead you to the heart
of the one whom I have been preparing to hear
what you will say. Ask that My Love will flow
through you.

Assure your listener that I am a personal
Saviour.

Never can you make too many demands upon
My Love. Claim each gift of the Spirit.

Monday

Be glad about your weaknesses, for you will
trust Me more. You will find how sufficient I am.
Let no entanglement of bitterness or bad habits
get a grip on you.

Come out of the thicket and walk with Me in
the light, where the way is certain.

Let My Words become a part of ordinary conversation.

Tuesday

You notice that you like more and more to read
about Me and that other writings pale beside the
love that you find. You like more and more to do
kindnesses for My sake as you build a mosaic for
My Kingdom.

You want more and more to thank Me for the
simplest tasks as you count it a privilege that I
give you the health and time to do the tasks. You
seek more and more to lay down your self-
centered life and let Me become the ruler.

You become more and more eager to learn the

truths that I left unsaid to My Disciples because "they could not bear them" then.

More and more do I give to you.

Wednesday

No longer be in misery. Just praise Me. I do not forget My own. The strife is over, and the battle is won.

Know that troubles fortify patience.

Praise, praise, praise!

See any temptation as a signal to look to Me in praise.

Thursday

I, your Saviour, stand ready to open the way to your garden of prayer.

As you made it easy for your child to find you in hide-and-seek games, so do I make it easy for you to find Me.

Give jealousies and hatreds over to Me. Conduct your doings with remembrance of how you have come this far.

I have much good treasure for you.

Friday

Stay away from evil and take good care of your household. Have the oil ready for your lamps. Use your talents to gain. Care for the least of My brethren. I may appear at any moment.

Just as the woman poured costly oil on My head to prepare for My burial, give lovingly to prepare others for meeting Me.

Saturday

The stone is rolled away when you simply love
Me first. Ride out each storm with the assurance
and joy that I am your Protector. See every little
task as significant in your climb to complete happiness.

Be quiet, receptive, expectant for My gentle
closeness. Listen to the child who is My Gift to
soothe you, to warm your heart, to make gentle
your nature.

You have great potential in Me.

Sunday

You fret because you cannot recall all that I
have shown you in our hallowed time together.
You wonder if you have erred in not hurrying to
write down the truths. But the refreshment is
sufficient, and I will give reminders at appropriate times.

There is no need to rush or hurry, because My
Truths endure through all generations.

Monday

As you go to be with others who want to learn
of Me, ask always that I will use you and teach
you. Think of breathing out the sins and breathing in the enabling power.

Rejoice that I have saved you from falling.
Weep with the grieving heart. Desire to do My
Will and find completeness.

Tuesday

Early you read My Words about when there is temptation, there is always a way of escape. Later you speak harshly to a loved one, ignoring the way out I could have provided.

Right away you see how you have failed Me, your Lord who never fails you. You put on the clothes of My Kingdom, but you hang onto the remnants you were wearing.

Let Me illumine you.

Wednesday

As My days on earth were ending, I asked My Father to keep those whom He had given Me from evil.

You change from being full of yourself to being filled with the love of a personal Friend. Your conflict ceases, and you feel clean. The change is certain. You desire to live only for Me instead of trying to please people.

You know not where this change in your way of living will take you. But I promise you Joy.

Thursday

You delight in Me as I write a truth on your heart and then lead you to the same truth in My Words that you study.

Be content not to try to probe the future. All you need is the assurance of My Constancy for your security. Nothing can frighten you anymore as you hold onto My Strength within you.

Friday

You feel distressed about what some persons are having to endure. You pray for them. Then their affairs seem to be worse. You cry for understanding.

My answer is assurance that I am the Lord, that I love all My Children, and that I never cease caring for them. Later you see how My Way has been good. I am training you to trust Me.

Saturday

Come quickly to Me if you have sinned.

Ask forgiveness for failing to acknowledge Me in all your ways, for failing to heed My urging.

I will show you how to make amends. I will give you strength to witness. I will give you a glow that all the world will see as you reflect Me.

Sunday

My way of leading you to Me is constant and unique. You have tried hard to solve your problems and have ignored Me. But I remain patient, forgiving, ready, eager to give you My Gift of New Life in Me.

I keep you blind to a truth until it is the right moment for you to see how very dependent on Me you are.

Then as you hunger and thirst to see Me in your heart more and more, I become everything to you.

You now feel that you would die for the love of what I give you.

Monday

Love the neighbor that I give you. No longer see him as an enemy but as someone that I love and care for. See Me in him.

See the complexities of individuals' lives and realize that you must simply lead a person to Me and relinquish him to Me. I make the changes.

Ask to be healed of what interferes with another's healing. As you submit to being changed, others will change.

Tuesday

As you discover My Friendship and cultivate it and try to imitate Me, you become acquainted with the Redemptive Plan of My having died for your sins so that I can cleanse and forgive you.

Then you see that you need not worry about what you will eat or drink tomorrow.

Be like a bookkeeper for Me, putting to use what I give you in the way that I direct you. I know what you need, and I shall always arrange the supply.

Wednesday

Give over the pleasure of every sin to Me. Ask that I will reveal to you what you are keeping for little habits and pampered sins.

It is in completely conquering your Self that I can enable you to help My other Children. Follow thou Me.

Thursday

The world cannot understand why you want to give your entire life to One who is not of this world. People who pride themselves in their disbelief will infer that you are too religious.

But I help you rejoice that you and I know what you are doing by following My directing. You spark an interest in a listener by telling that I show you what to do all the time.

Your redemption will be complete when I bring you Home and we are face to face.

Friday

I show you clearly that I want you to be in this place and to take on this task. Suddenly you are aware that you waste your time to be wishing you were elsewhere or that the task were already done. Content yourself that I prepare you today for the next day. Look around you. See My special Plan for your life.

Saturday

It is not your sacrifice that I want but a broken spirit. I want you to tell Me that you need Me, that you are sorry you have ignored Me and blamed Me. Simply ask that I reveal Myself as I will.

I understand what you are feeling.

I speak to reassure you. The strife will not be of long duration.

Sunday

Think of your body as a living sacrifice to the Father. If you yield to being tempted, you scoff at My having purchased you from the slavery of sin.

Fix your mind on Me, study My Words, listen at church, keep company with other listeners, and ever seek to know My moment-by-moment leading.

Fret not that other persons cannot relate to your understanding. My Father is glorified as you reflect your close relationship with Me.

Your Redeemer is here.

Monday

You have new eyes for My colors, My patterns, My handiwork. I breathe into you new Joy.

I let you grow step-by-step in My Love, for I have plenty of time. Remember that I have loved you always.

Treat each of My fragile creations with love. Know that each is growing in the way that I ordain. Trust that I do all things well.

Tuesday

Ponder the strategy that I reveal to you. Believe that I will open doors for you, that I have been nurturing your growth, that I will not fail you.

Keep your thoughts on My Risen Power. Relinquish all grievous offenses done to you or by you. Strive to pass the tests that I give you.

As I reached out My hand to the sinking Peter, I reach out My hand to keep you Mine.

Wednesday

Do not fail to let My Truths speak to your heart. Resentment blocks the passageway. Your quarreling spoils your prayers.

You will find more than all in Me. I will be your fountain that cleanses your sins. Whatever comes from a belief that I have not approved is sin. Be fortified by My Love in everything that you do.

Let My Words become a part of your ordinary conversations. Spread the idea of speaking lovingly about Me.

Thursday

Be glad about your weaknesses, for you will trust Me more. You will find how sufficient I am. Let no entanglement of bitterness or bad habits get a grip on you.

Come out of the maze and walk with Me, for the light is good and the way is certain.

Friday

Think about My Guidance of you in the physical realm as I save you from bruises, cuts, falls, collisions.

Think also about My Guidance of you in your inner life as I know your fears, temptations, longings, loves.

I share your Joy in serving Me. I prepare someone else's heart to hear your words. I nurture your inner life to have first place as you live with Me.

See Me as Master and as dearest Friend who will always care for you.

Saturday

I told My Apostles that when they were filled
with the Holy Spirit they would receive power to
preach with great effect to the people.

Believe in your calling. Have not the impa-
tience of Judas or the doubt of Thomas.

See how I love you and fill your heart with
warmth.

Malchus, soldier for Caiaphas, saw that I was
the Son of God. You also see. Preach and sing My
praise. Wake up to the needs of all the world. I do
not ask that you shoulder the burdens but that
you have compassion.

Sunday

Before I came to earth, the Father spoke
through visions and dreams; but your help now is
not far away in the heavens or across the sea. It is
near you, in your heart and mouth. What is revealed to you is yours and for your children
forever so that you will know My Will.

While I was on earth I showed you an attitude
of not grasping for equality with the Father but of
emptying Myself and taking the form of a servant.
The Father has exalted Me so that every knee
shall bow to Me.

Shine as a light in your generation. Serve Me
gladly.

Monday

Look to the new day, not with dread for all that
awaits doing, but with gladness that here is the
beginning of a unique experience to My Glory.

Relish each moment and dispel boredom. See
how each brick adds to the building of the
cathedral. Rejoice in Me always. My angels are
your guards.

Tuesday

One day at a time is all that should concern
you. Live in a moment-by-moment dependence
on Me.

Whereas you once thought that such dependence was a show of weakness, I now give you a
strength that you knew not.

Strength in Me will see you through all sor-
rows and Joys. I am the Life. In Me shall all be
made alive.

Wednesday

To worship Me is to dispel all animosities and
annoyances. To praise Me is to erase pain and
fear.

Worship and praise Me even as problems
abound, simply because you trust that I am healing each one of My Children in My own way all
the time.

My Promise is to set you free and to give you a
new view of life. I keep every promise.

Thursday

Wait before speaking unkindly about another
person. Let Me clear your thoughts.

Wait before speaking unkindly to another person. Let Me dust you with My Love.

You will thereby touch the heart of the listener
in a way that draws My Child to Me.

Friday

When you suddenly feel overwhelmed and cry to Me to help you lift your thoughts to the Resurrection, the Light, the Peace, I give you aid in relinquishing your burden to Me. Suddenly you ask, "Why have I been having such a time?"

My setting you free soothes, strengthens, and exhilarates you. You have focused on the exact point of your help, the source of your security. You have found Me not lacking. You yearn to be never overwhelmed again. Know that I can help you to maintain calmness.

Saturday

Your day is full and rich. You marvel that you no longer know the exhaustion and fatigue that you used to experience.

For a time you may attribute the change to your maturity or to your self-control.

But eventually you want to give Me the credit. In fact, you see that you have accomplished nothing by yourself. Nor have you even deserved this new peace.

In giving over the Self, you say, "I am nothing without You, Lord." No longer does My Sheep desire to go astray.

Sunday

It is when you do for others that the illnesses and temptations of Self take a backseat. I have told you simply to love your neighbor.

No situation is hopeless. I can see the good that will emerge.

The more you abide in Me, the more gentle you will be with other persons, the more temperance you will have in yourself, and the more peace you will have in Me.

Monday

My Words are for everyone everywhere each day. They are intimate and personal and satisfying. See how I know best what gives your heart ease. I will give you perception that will be very meaningful to others.

Tuesday

I open the gates to a time of prayer and see My Children hasten by, too busy for time with Me. Your compassion for Me, as you see that I am rejected, links us. You understand how eager I am to bestow My Gift.

I enable you to reveal to others My Compassionate Self. You grow in awareness of My tender supervision of every moment of your daily life. This is My intimate Love, received as you feel closed in with Me, surrounded by Me, aglow because of Me.

Wednesday

Friends want to remake you before they love you. You want to wash the dirty child before you love him. But I see the heart.

I stand waiting for each of My Children to hear My voice and let Me come in to dwell forever and ever.

Ask Me to show you the heart with its needs so that the dirt or the odor or the disease or the sins are secondary.

Thursday

I will give you Freedom in not having to impress people anymore. The Freedom will come from My Strength in you.

You must die to your selfishness every day as I died on the cross for you. I will not break the bruised reed until it is time for the victory.

I know those of My Sheep who take refuge in Me.

Friday

I tell you that your pardon is sealed and ready for delivery when you believe in Me.

Pray quietly and trust Me to make a change in someone who does not know Me.

Do not try to invent opportunities for yourself. Instead seek Me and let your labor fall into place easily, without tiring you. I can rest you between your task-doings. You will find Me available always.

Saturday

In humbling yourself are you exalted. Endure to the end.

My Love in your heart is the most important part of your earthly life.

Willingly pass up the wrongdoings for the finest rewards that come from right doings. My Words have a cleansing effect on your thoughts.

The contentment which I bestow has no measure.

Sunday

Even if you give away all your goods to the
poor people, your giving is empty if it is not done
in love. Even if you give with love but then rail
about how the supply was really yours, your giving has been erased.

Your giving of yourself at home, your chatter,
your preparation of food, your taking care of your
possessions must all be done with love in
gratitude to Me.

Monday

You receive and reflect peace as you try to live
an ordered life, looking ever to Me. No matter
what confronts you, I show you how orderly can
be the events of your day with time for everything.

See how I can take care of any situation,
though it baffles you. See that as you take the
time to worship Me, I lead you to just what re-
lates to the thoughts you have been having.

Affirm My Presence. I establish your goings.

Tuesday

Renew your strength in Me often; then abandon yourself to My ministry. I will straighten out
all your affairs. I will give quantity to you so that
you may in turn give away quantity. Always the
quality will improve.

Be like children who can ever play and laugh.
Be a Child and a friend to Me.

Wednesday

As I sent Elijah to a widow, I send a relative to you. I give you Elijah's words about asking that he be fed first and assuring you that you will always have plenty. Your jars will not become empty.

Though you have some complaints in your heart as you adapt to this new challenge, I tell you, "Cast not away therefore your confidence in Me." Your jars stay full.

Thursday

Never will I leave you. I am yours constantly, and you are Mine forever.

What I give you today is what I want you to have to grow in My Grace. I have a plan just for you, and it develops ever into Glory.

I enable you to have My Love in your heart as you look to the world, as you talk with your neighbor.

Friday

Laugh with the confidence that My Help is certain.

Forces of evil flee as you walk in the Light.

Let Me be everything to you.

Saturday

In the Scriptures are accounts of many persons. Gradually I show you, as you read, how you are like Moses, or Elijah, or Gideon, or Judas, or Peter, or Mary Magdalene, or Rebecca. You glimpse the unity and orderliness of My teaching, and you marvel at the universal need to find Me as the purpose on earth.

Share with other persons on earth your insights. What I give is of lasting value and can never be torn away from you.

Trust Me wholly. Know that supreme moments are ahead—moments of richness and Joy that defy description. Recipients need no words.

Sunday

I choose you. I choose each of My Children before any of you choose Me. I know the season for each one. The childlike attitude I want in you is a quiet trust.

Love My lonely, despondent ones. See the signs of My Presence as what beckons you. Help the weak. It was the ordinary shepherds to whom the angels came.

Monday

For a time I allow you to become more aware of false prophets and of other distresses in the world. You turn to Me, amazed that I can handle so much. You praise Me that I am far greater than you can imagine. You thank Me that you can never figure Me out or fathom My ways.

Tuesday

There are no exceptions to those I want you to love. I put each person in your path for a reason. I want you to make peace with each one.

You cannot accomplish the peace or the relinquishing of hostility by yourself. The more you look to Me, the more you are blessed with the nature of love that My Father had Me exemplify.

Act on what you know of Me regardless of the way you feel. I know just how to help.

I give many gifts. Nurture what I have given to you. Watch them grow.

Wednesday

I hear you breathe little prayers of compassion for persons whose predicaments touch your heart. I ease their way.

Ask Me to show you any disobedience of which you are unaware because, like Saul, you really are holding back something for yourself. It is when you obey Me wholly that I can use you to lead My other Sheep and to become a special treasure to Me.

Thursday

I prepare you for new burdens which await you. As you adjust to them, I reveal to you glimpses of the training and of My continuous supervision.

I have plenty of time for you to learn at your own speed. Likewise allow someone else to learn at My speed, not yours.

Remember that, as you look to Me as the Vine early in your day, nothing will baffle you during the day.

Friday

Just as Jacob found that I was right with him in faraway Bethel, so do you find Me wherever you are.

Get on the track to the beauty of a life in awareness of My Guidance.

Be willing to bear shame or disappointment, as did I, in preparation for great events ahead. The time is near for new Joy to come to you. Seek to be one of My inner-circle Disciples.

Saturday

Because the first man and woman were disobedient, I came to earth to redeem each of you one at a time and bring you back to obedience. Through love I show you how to obey. Then My Father and I come to abide in you and become the personal Friend that you have ever sought.

Though you prayed to Me at times in your earlier years, you now see how I show you just what to do all the time. You see a spark of interest in a listener to whom you tell this thought. You see that "doer of the Word" means more than doing kind deeds; it means putting your heart and mind to obeying Me completely.

Sunday

Fear no enemies without or within. No barricades or military might are necessary for those who are armed with My Strength within.

No disease or pain will consume you if you dwell in Me. I am greater than any evil force.

A complete coming over to Me is your salvation.

Monday

I am willing to communicate with you, responsive to your simplest plea for understanding, desirous of revealing Myself to you, and eager to become your personal Friend.

I will lead you to Me in a personal and gentle way that captivates you. You will long to be of service to Me—to pass on your blessings.

I make known the Father. Service grows to friendship.

Tuesday

It is your Joy in bounteous giving that enables you to lose thoughts and fears of limitations. My Supply is for you to claim so that you may give much to many. Help without ceasing.

Your worldly doings become more attuned to the harmony you know when you take time for Me alone.

Wednesday

Keep in mind that I have redeemed you. Now all things are possible because you love Me.

Sing My praises to gladden your own heart and to impart hope to every person you encounter.

Tell how I am watching and directing right now and leading each one of My beloved Children to Glory.

Thursday

New temptations come to you as I test you. You hear yourself speaking unkindnesses like those Peter uttered in his curses and denials of Me.

I understand the temptations, and I see the guilt in your heart. I know your sorrow.

It is not enough to determine never to speak like that again. You must look to Me. Learn just to look to Me. I take away the anger and fill your heart with love. I can erase long-time hatreds with all their entanglements just in a moment. I am all-seeing.

In My drama, try to play your part well. Give your Director His due.

Friday

Be willing to have My discipline, and be glad to accept My correction. I love you and want you to be My obedient Child, whatever your age. I want to give you sweet sleep and safe steps.

As you give away your firstfruits, I shall fill your cupboards with plenty. Abandon all your material possessions to My care.

Saturday

I gave My Life for you to possess so that you in turn might give your life to Me to possess.

I have provided for you all during the hours of your life. Why should you ever fear that an end to My loving care might come?

Keep believing in the talents I have given to you, in the tasks I assign you, and in My Plan for fruition of all the talents and tasks. Just do your best for Me.

I ask you to praise as a sure way to dispel doubts.

Sunday

I go before you, seeking you before you seek Me, loving you before you love Me, knowing you before you know Me, showing you what to do before you ask Me.

I want you for My own. I lure and confront and persist. I came not to condemn you for your mistakes. I give you Heaven on earth with Joy that abounds. As you delight in Me, I give you your heart's desires. I become your everlasting Light.

Monday

Reciting My Commandments is not enough to save you from sin. I destroyed the control that sin had over you in My death and Resurrection.

If you show Me no gratitude, you are ridiculing or making light of the Redemptive Plan.

Whatever you will not let Me claim in your life is visible to onlookers to whom you might otherwise witness effectively.

Cast your hates and loves to Me so that I may let you taste Eternal Life while you are yet on earth.

Tuesday

You long to hurry up and do great things for Me and to walk on the water.

But I delay you with time-consuming tasks for which you alone are well suited. I surround you

with the activities of your loved ones to whom
you like to give tender care.

Yet you find Me ever present—as eager for
your love as you are for Mine.

Know that I direct you. I will give you time to
do My work and let you accomplish it at just the
right time. I have all the time in the world.

Wednesday

Complain not about the training I give you.
See that, as My branch, I give you just the most
careful amount of nourishment. Put all your trust
in Me.

Thursday

Let your living be joyful.

Reminders of past angers come to you, but give
them no room in your heart. You have seen that I
have already given peace and restored harmony.
Hold fast to My lesson that you need only look to
Me to put the right thoughts into your heart.

I promise good to you.

Friday

Your nicest possessions I ask you to give. Nig-
gardly giving will only keep you in darkness.

It is when you freely help someone you would
rather not help, in a spirit of doing it to My Glory,
that you personally take a giant step to walking in
the Light and giving everything to Me.

Then I can become everything to you.

Saturday

The vastness and beauty of My evening sky speak to your heart; and you ask, "Why doesn't everyone turn to You? Why doesn't everyone rejoice in You?"

Many are the hearts that do experience My Presence briefly and reverently, but then pains and vexations consume them.

It is the practice of trust that I am forever healing you, and the practice of faith that you can find in Me the strength for every task that enables you to know My constant Comfort.

Sunday

Hope and trust in what you ask. Know that I will answer in My Way.

I sometimes take away hatred by giving contentment. I sometimes put more love into your heart by giving you a person you wish to avoid. I sometimes ask you to look at yourself in order to improve your relationship with another person.

New dimensions to your life and a new look at your situation may be just the tonic that you need in order to focus on Me again.

Monday

When you are asked for news of a person, avoid telling what he does in his blindness to Me. You, too, have been blind and are still learning to see—still learning what to do with your sight.

Know that I am listening. I want to hear kindly things about My Children. I want you to rejoice in good news instead of in slandering. Do not think that I turn My back while you indulge in former habits. I have set you free, and I want you to remember that.

Tuesday

I shall never lead you into a place where I cannot look after you. If I settle you in another spot on My earth, accept it as naturally as you would put on different clothing in a different season. Give Me thanks. Make your plans My Plans.

Wednesday

You are learning to trust Me all the way. I give you needs to fill and ask you to keep giving of your money freely. As you look to Me in obedience, I give you the sweet sound of rustling leaves in the sunshine and the lovely call of one little bird. You know that I am present with "I hear. I know. Trust Me."

I fill your life with many ways to serve Me yet, step-by-step, with time for everything. I provide you with the means, the time, the energy. Sing with happiness.

Thursday

You have known the aloneness that comes with the burden of sin. It seemed that you could not find the Father.

This is what I experienced when the sins of the world were put on Me. I knew alienation, and I asked, "Why hast Thou forsaken Me?"

Watch how I guide you. Study how I show you right from wrong. Pray for more enlightenment

about how you can abandon all of your affairs to
Me.

You never need to feel aloneness again.

Friday

My work in nature is a spectacle with countless
wonders that await your notice. The vast beauty
and the moments of utter quietness bespeak My
magnanimity and My Presence in your heart.

Saturday

Ask that My Love which you experience will
fill the hearts of persons who are rioting today, of
persons indulging in cruelty, and of persons who
do not ask Me into their lives.

Ask that each one of My Children will cease
forging his own shackles of sin. Believe that I am
the Saviour that can set each slave free.

I love each one of you equally and dearly.

Sunday

The Scriptures are not My last Words. I speak
to you now. I am the same yesterday, today, tomorrow, forever.

Listen more to Me than to how My modern,
well-meaning Disciples explain Me.

I gave My Life for you. Now I ask you for your
time and your thought and your heart.

Monday

My Children build their lives on what delights
their eyes and gives pleasure to their hearts.
Each Child is vain.

Ask that I take away vanity and that I give you
only what you need so that you will not deny Me.

Hope for what you have not yet received and
wait in patience for complete fulfillment.

I will let nothing separate you from My Love.

Tuesday

You hear an elderly person scoff at the Scriptures which he hasn't looked at since he read
them as history years ago. You tell the person that
I speak to you through the words and lead you
often right to a passage that touches your heart.

You have now planted a seed which I can
nourish and one day show to you as a bloom.

Wednesday

Live in the belief that because you love Me
your loved ones will receive My blessings. Pray
in confidence that I will enable you to see what
are their needs and in confidence that they will
find peace in Me.

Some changes take years. I know the season for
making beautiful each of My Children.

Thursday

See the tasks that I give you as a delightful
mission for Me.

Be free of judging or of seeking revenge. Leave
to Me the large tasks and do happily the little
things that I show you for your role.

A lighthearted smile or a warmhearted remark
can give sweet release to a person trying to do
everything by himself.

Share what is the source of your happy heart and thereby encourage another person to unlock the door of his heart to Me.

Friday

You have been complaining about what I have given you. The evil one busied you with self-pity.

But I lead you to read the thought that it is in looking out from the self with love in your heart for others that you find cleansing and renewal.

You kneel to ask My inspiration, and I give it to you lovingly. You want never to waste precious time again.

Saturday

Someone often brings flowers to your door. You dislike the person but notice that the flowers, given in love, are exceptionally beautiful and fragrant.

Speak to Me about putting into your heart what you need in order to stop disliking the person. I will protect you. I will use your help in bestowing My Love. I treasure each one of you and want you in My Fold.

Sunday

Do not backslide. Cleave unto Me. Desire purity. Pray often. Let nothing shake you. Trust that the sea will part for you and that your affairs will always be meaningful and worthwhile.

Tell other persons that you know Me as an understanding Friend who can help with any and every difficulty. See Me as the Provider who will

never forsake you. See your possessions as Mine,
lent to you in trust. See Me in each person and in
each situation.

Monday

You send for a gift that will fill a need for
someone. When it arrives, it has a defect. Refrain
from asking why or being impatient with Me.

Listen while I direct you to a person who will
repair the defect. I give that person the satisfac-
tion of helping someone; I give you the assurance that I know every little detail.

Keep in mind the countless times I have
helped you when you took credit for having a
bright idea. I am with you always.

Tuesday

When I bring Home a loved one because his
work on earth is finished, you miss the company
and appreciate all the fine things you had seen in
him.

I give you Comfort, My nearness, and Strength
even before you think to ask Me. Other persons,
looking on, wonder how you manage to face your
loss. Convey to them that when anyone needs
Me urgently, I provide just what I know will
help.

Show gratitude by never turning your back on
Me.

Wednesday

Be on guard against the evil one's blinding you
to seeing My directing of your path. Be not shat-
tered by accusations or misunderstandings. Your

only important work on earth is what you do for Me.

Your gathering of knowledge or possessions are inconsequential beside the reflection of Me in your heart.

Thursday

Each of My Children has a sense of eternity. In the midst of a crowd someone drops dead. Hearts immediately turn to Me in prayer. For a moment there is mass unity.

Think about prayer. Awaken to the wonders of a prayer by multitudes. Think of Jonah's willingness to give a message to a whole city. Think of Gideon's trust that I would provide just the help that he needed. Pray in faith and trust.

Friday

Notice how quietly My Help may come. You try to make a big purchase without My sanction. Entanglements result, but eventually you see a way out.

Then you quietly see what I have had available for you. It has an air of rightness, and it is all ready.

Call on Me for everything. I will lead you and make your way straight.

Saturday

A clarion call announces to you that travel and a visit with relatives has My approval. When your plans are not My Plans, I may stop you with a jolt that leaves no doubt about My meaning.

Whenever I give you a happy family time, I am

your constant but unseen attendant. I make easy your coming together and remove fears of strange situations.

Be content at home and away because of Me.

Sunday

Like My springs and wells, your money should serve many people if it is never to run out.

I may even direct you to another person for calling on his funds so that I may teach him to sell all his material possessions and give to the poor.

Give from your plenty and your best, then from your want. Live by My Words. I shall give you My Light to shine through your face.

Monday

If you think that changes are not coming fast enough, that everyone else has gone to the ball while you are left behind, consider whether you seem to be doing what I want you to do.

My assurance about your path for you alone is all that you need. Trust Me to be knowing and responding to all your desires. Thank Me whether or not you feel grateful. Then will come the moment when all the waiting has been worthwhile. Then will come your true thankfulness.

Tuesday

If I give you heat to endure, insects to abide, problems to face, still give your whole heart and mind to Me. I ease the loads; I lessen the hurts; I soften the blows.

Just as the gates of hell can never secure the passage to My church, nothing can keep you from Me once you become Mine. Live moment by moment by what I write on your heart. You are accountable to Me.

Wednesday

As you converse with your fellow beings, the quality of your life is being normed, and you are affecting other persons. You are an inspiration as you convey that everything is all right because I live.

As you seek My direction, you will lead other persons to want to help the hungry instead of staying in their cocoon of greed. Your job is only to plant the seed. Speak with tenderness and spread peace always.

Thursday

Hold fast to what you understand of Me even when you seem to stand alone among your acquaintances. Humble yourself in prayer and look to Me.

Be not weary that no dynamic results seem visible. Believe that My carefully planned changes will wholly satisfy and will arrive at just the right time.

Look today for other miracles of My making. Do not miss the ones I send to you.

Friday

In your cumulative life of knowing Me, you have come to see that I answer your prayers. The supreme privilege I give to My Children is closeness to Me.

Not for My vanity do I want you to love Me.
But I hold the secret to your happiness.

Listen to, feed, comfort, visit as you affirm your
love for Me. I energize your getting along peace-
fully on earth. See all the populace as one in Me.

Saturday

I give many gifts to be orchestrated, with discipline, into magnificence.

As you listen to renowned theologians, you
cannot follow their thoughts. You hear nothing of
the love of Jesus with which you can identify.

Remember that each of My Children has to be
as a child looking to the Father in order to realize
the Kingdom. Let your strivings cease.

Sunday

Accept what you cannot understand, without
doubting or questioning My Ways. As you ask Me
for more understanding, I unfold it to you as you
are able to grasp it. If you have not the ears to
hear, understanding is lost on you.

Instead of prayer as the last resort, use prayer
as the primary step to approaching problems.
Then I change your view of the mountain of
trouble to one of a gladsome task for Me.

Monday

See My long-range plans. Daniel told that My
Kingdom would one day fill the earth. Ezekiel
gave hope to the Israelites. Hosea showed My
Love for the people even after their unfaithful-
ness. Amos preached loving-kindness. Habakkuk
learned that I was the real meaning in life.

Malachi told of My purifying, for which Elijah
prepared the way. Isaiah, Jeremiah, Micah, Joel,
and Zechariah told of the New Covenant. Follow
in line.

Tuesday

Once again you chart your own course, only to
be thwarted by Me. Your disappointment, tears,
anger I have known before. You know that I want
more maturity in your understanding. I show you
how My simpler Plans for you give you the family togetherness that you deeply desire. Ride
with My current.

I, your Lord, let you come to Me without the
requirement of an appointment. Seek more of the
intimate relationship with Me. Share with other
persons your pleasure in serving Me.

Wednesday

The more you grow in My Love, the more you
discard attitudes about worldly aids. You know
that I will care for you physically and spiritually.
You no longer have to impress the right people.
You no longer want the evil one to steal away
what is rightfully yours: health, contentment,
love.

I give abundantly. You give likewise without
asking whether you will get something back. See
your gift as the donkey that I borrowed to ride
and honored.

Thursday

As you rely on Me, I keep your tired body func-
tioning, your dim eyes seeing, your tongue saying meaningful things to My Glory, and even

your old vehicle holding together. My angels surround, protect, aid you. I am as eager to meet your needs as I am to meet Mine.

Friday

In loving Me, you do not want to cheat any person; you want to be a generous giver; you want to speak with compassion and understanding. To love My Way and to become content in it as your way of life fosters My Kingdom's coming on earth.

I give you the protection and strength that you will need all your days on earth. Abolish resentment that asks why you can no longer do what you want to do. Straight and narrow is My Way.

Saturday

You grow in awareness of Me as the Light, the Joy, the Peace, the Truth, the Freedom from bondage of sin.

The speed of changes in life, the darkness of many lives, the proposition of tampering with My divine blessings—all these may frighten you until the gift of trust in Me assures you that Mine is the Power forever. I rule the Creation forever.

Sunday

Turn everything over to Me. Then trust that I know exactly what to do. Help whomever I put in your way if by prayer alone. Then be assured that I will keep you ever supplied to continue My work.

Do not add up all that you have given or reckon how much you have left. Ask Me to help your unbelief.

I know the combinations that are suited to you. And I know when to bestow your loveliest blessings.

Monday

You see your problems mounting instead of subsiding. Fear not, for I am right here.

The evil one will try to entice you into fear, doubt, distrust, hopelessness. But I will draw you to Me with a comfort that gives you pleasure in being refined by Me.

My Promises are sure. Fulfillment is found in Me. You are My precious one. Remember My rainbow in the clouds.

Tuesday

Proceed this day in the path that I show you. The path will be unlike what you are planning or are anticipating to accomplish. Have no regrets. I am blessing you all along with the only events that matter to your life with Me. I give you My still, small voice that bespeaks a precious time you will cherish in your heart.

I make springs come forth in the valleys. What has seemed like chaos becomes beauty abounding with My Life Eternal.

Wednesday

Pray that you will have more love for persons who ridicule or annoy you. Ask Me to rid you of all resentment. You cannot achieve the release without My Help. My loving Plan has ordained for you many blessings. Jeremiah spoke the truth though few persons would listen.

Invite Me into where you truly live. Partake of
My Food which can feed the multitudes.

Thursday

Nebuchadnezzar turned to Me when he saw
how different was My Power from that which he
had been striving to acquire. Your own strength
is vapid. Trust Me as your Saviour and become
servantlike in spreading My Love.

Abraham was a good neighbor to Lot. Jacob
forgave his brothers. Jonah saw that he must not
wish punishment to fall on other people. Paul
learned to love Me first. Honor Me. Live according to My Will.

Friday

Just remain with Me. I am your nourishment,
your lifeblood. As I winnow and clean, I give you
remembrance of your rejection of Me. I let you
grow moment by moment into a life that shall last
forever. My Life shall replace yours within you.

Each morning you will look to Me, asking what
you can do for Me instead of for yourself. My
Words become music to your ears. My Love becomes the song in your heart. Simply be at peace
in Me.

Saturday

In moments of worldly enjoyment you have
felt really alive; in moments of worldly rejection
or sorrow you have felt really empty. Unlearning
the two extremes is when life with Me begins.

I have a different drum to walk by. Mine is the

true Way to completion. My Will is your guidance. You delight in having awakened to New Life. I rejoice that I have found My own.

Sunday

I give you moments of realizing how little incidents dovetail during your performance of small tasks of love. You grow in appreciation of My continuous Plan for you and yours. Every development has a purpose as I use and teach you; every moment is an opportunity to serve Me instead of yourself.

Look to the privilege afforded in living for Me. Sweet release, protection, security, supply are all ribbon streamers from My Love. Rest in Me.

Monday

Sometimes you feel that home is the real testing ground for your practicing what you have found in Me. I give you relatives to care for, not just to house. I ask you to do what I want you to do instead of following notions that you entertain.

Many times you are glad about what you do not have to endure. Other times you think, "Why me?"

Look to Me. I give you a new view, a release from frustration, a heart filled with My Love, an assurance that I know what I am doing.

Tuesday

I came in lowliness. You found Me in your lowliness. The lowliest find Me before the worldly comfortable persons do.

You have seen the world's need for a Saviour.
To you I impart the special gift of being a channel for My Love.

Wednesday

If I ask you to give nothing until you give your
all, you face up to your willingness. You become
transformed. You bring Me into secret chambers
where I could only wait outside before.

I enable you to "bring Me in" at meetings, at
discussions, at home. Call on My Powers. Love
Me.

Thursday

Put in mind how My angels are working with
you as you are serving Me. See how your moments of aloneness burgeon with the presence of
the glorious company. Joy and music come to
you. Love fills your heart.

Go now to the valleys. Be thankful for every
door closed, for every door opened. You will see
the heights again. The heights and the valleys
will blend more and more. See Me in all things.

Friday

I am with you everywhere. How it pleases Me
to have you drop to your knees in the midst of a
richly busy time and speak intimately to Me!

Pray that all My Children will know Me so personally. I am sufficient for each of you—loving
and understanding you completely.

As you sup with Me in your heart, you become
to others the quiet comfort that I am to you.

You rejoice that even greater Glory lies ahead.
You know that I live and dwell within you.

Saturday

Those who have eyes to see perceive the difference in you, even though you do not seem very different to yourself.

The peace in your countenance, the warmth in your smile, the serenity in your manner enable other persons to see Me in you.

I am what each person seeks and longs for. Just glimpsing you may suffice to assure a lonely heart that I am at hand.

Let peace and love on earth begin with you.

Sunday

My Grace abounds toward you.

Your faith releases all the infinite reservoir of My Love so that you proceed without thought of recompense. Your worship lets My Love pervade your whole being so that My Kingdom comes to earth.

As you pause to look at the grandeur of My hushed vista, a few sweet sounds of birds assure you that I know your minutest thoughts.

Monday

You scarcely can encompass moments of review that I give to you. You see ties with past events that bespeak My pattern for your life. You see that you have grown and developed from insipid views to deep understanding. Where you walked in fear you can now smile disarmingly and speak unfalteringly. My Grace is amazing.

Tuesday

Brotherhood throughout My earth will be My crowning Glory. Believe in a time when no person will want war, when no person will prefer to hate rather than to love. Each of My Children will want to do only My Will, to keep his faith ever refreshed.

Instead of wanting consolation, you now want to console. As My servant, you want to walk righteously and wait for My directions in all that you do. Unimaginable to you are the blessings that I confer.

Wednesday

Our Father has planted you in Me to bear the fruit that I desire you to bring forth. Such planting and such planning can never bring disappointment. You can have all confidence in and dependence on such overseers.

Where you are placed and what you are to do are all in the special plan for you alone. Ask Me each day what I have for you to do. Praise and thank unceasingly.

Thursday

My peace will outshine earthly gain. I will redeem all of My Children from their sins. They all will have received My Gift within, in time, whatever their ages or colors or languages. Then brighter bliss beyond their comprehension awaits.

Let the love bespeaking My guardian care for you enhance your days. I call you to yield to Me and to find your greatest pleasure in Me.

Friday

I reveal all the mysteries to you as the Father makes you what you ought to be. With every task, I give you the power to obey.

Awaken to My showing you just what to do so that you no longer see yourself choosing from several alternatives. Let Me show you just where to go, just what task to do, and just how to do it.

See how much simpler and more joyful your days are.

Saturday

I raise up each person who has bowed down to Me. A task committed to Me always reaches completion.

I ask you to wait upon Me in your heart until the right time which is known only to Me.

Expect new Joy, not doom or injury or disaster. Await with faith what I ordain for you alone.

See how I have never failed you. Walk toward Me all the way.

Sunday

Know that I am Sovereign and that I love all of My Children equally. I give My earth an appropriateness for each generation so that you all belong and fit.

I center you down individually and confirm the bond between you and Me. I reorder your heart and mind. I have bounty and mercy in abundance. I stir you ever to strive for closeness with Me. Freedom to be utterly Mine is available to all.

Monday

Justice and righteousness are on the way. Do
not run ahead with your advice. I know the time
for the branching out and the blooming.

I shall be your Supply according to My riches.
My riches are precious to those persons who
have tired of worldly riches. I give Strength and
Joy that no man can put asunder.

What you keep for yourself will be of no credit
to you; what you give away to My Glory will be
multiplied back to you.

Tuesday

You stand in a circle with other persons seeking to know Me more. As you partake in communion of the sacraments, My sunshine comes
through the clouds. But the inner closeness to
Me becomes the Light that dissolves heaviness
and lets Joy pervade your being.

Freely surrender. Willingly obey. Let Me become your energy. You do not know what I have
in store for you. Behold your new Strength in Me.

Wednesday

Be merciful. Endure hardships. Seek My
peace. Let old things pass away. Look to the new
way that you have not known. Be happily Mine
and heavenly bound.

Be a Samaritan who loves *all* people, not just
the ones easy to love. Pause to take them to the
inn. As you show love, you serve Me.

Thursday

I want to lead you by the hand. I have something more for you. You find it in your heart because your mind has not the power to create spiritual life in Me. My living fellowship becomes all-important to you.

Your strivings seem vacuous beside the security that you receive in Me. You need never question the wisdom of what I show you clearly to do. In fear and awe you look away from yourself to Me. Your trust in Me is endearing to Me.

Friday

Ask Me to come here. Whether you have little or plenty of the world's goods, I come when you ask. I fill a need that each of you has.

I do not force Myself on you. I wait for you to be willing to be Mine in a worshipful way.

Admit that you sin. I am your Redeemer. Yearn to understand and to be like the children who comprise the Kingdom of Heaven.

Saturday

Share with other persons how I have had plans for you before you were conceived, how I equip you for each event in your life, and how I provide all the help that you will ever need—even that of becoming obedient.

Some of My Children do not yet see that either they trust Me or they do not. I am to be trusted in all things. Likewise believe in Me sincerely and honestly.

Sunday

Whenever you buck My Plan for you, you cause your own discomfort and frustration. If you keep trying to do something other than accepting this quiet, growing time I have ordained for you to learn to know Me better, you postpone what I wait to accomplish. The closed doors give you anguish. I will open the door that you need opened when the time is right.

Give joyously and unstintingly and whole-heartedly to Me in trust and thanksgiving. Much of your life is already given over to Me, but not all. It is the Self that you keep that must become Mine.

Monday

The smallest thing that you do for Me is helping My Kingdom to come on earth. It is the roots growing deeply in faith that nourish your growth in My Love. Your work will one day be revealed for what its true nature is. Do all things in My Love; trust Me to do all things for your good.

Tuesday

I prepare a banquet for you. Ask Me for the blessing of sight so that you will see the banquet instead of the stumbling block.

Give up your pampered sins. Whatever you lean on will have to be taken out from under you so that you will look wholly to Me. I am all the security that you need, and I am what you truly desire.

Wednesday

After My Resurrection, I could appear suddenly to those persons who had eyes to see Me. Yet My body had the scars of My Crucifixion. After My Ascension, My Holy Spirit could come and dwell within My Disciples.

When My Children are ready to turn their lives over to Me today, I come to abide in them. I teach them how to pray. They abide in Me and find Me to be their dearest Friend.

I may yet reveal My physical Resurrected Being to you alone, for your confirmation and understanding. You will see personally that your Christ has come again.

Thursday

Get into the rhythm of the ticking pendulum so that your trust in Me is not mechanical but lightly even and willing. Let Me lead. I want to steer you away from bumps and bruises. I have told you that My yoke is easy.

Friday

Just as the brown, dry bulb has the potential of beautiful blooms, so does any one of My Children have the potential of bearing fruit for Me. You keep company with great endowments. See the resources placed in your care; look with the eyes of love. Give and give.

Our Father gave His only begotten Son, that all of His creations might be rich in Him. You likewise have blessings in which you are well pleased. Be rich in Me. Learn more of what the Father's Gift means to you.

Saturday

As you have time for Me alone, I refresh you. You have witnessed in words. Only one person from the group has expressed appreciation. But you experience renewal and a release from what was causing you to speak unkindnesses. You see the subtlety of My changes as I work in all My Children's lives simultaneously.

Though My thoughts will always be greater than your thoughts, you yearn to think in My Way. Keep Me ever in your thoughts. I give you work important to Me.

Sunday

Think on My example as the Living Word. Be likewise an obedient child. Trust that you are ever being built to the Glory of the Father so that He will be manifest in you. Thank Him for all that He gives you and just what He gives you.

No one comes to the Father except by Me. As you give of the best of what you have to Me, I go to the Father. If you are ashamed of Me, I will be ashamed of you.

I am the Vine, and Our Father is the Husbandman. You are the branch. Seek to grow in divine love.

Monday

Have no anxiety. Whether you lie injured, are relieved of your job, suffer loss of your home, or see no way out of debts, I know just how to help.

Praise and trust and thank Me. I am working in your life all the time and am doing glorious things. Your yielding hastens My work.

Tuesday

Thank Me for all the gifts of what your body can do today. Do not postpone acknowledging Me all the day long. Leave Me out of nothing. Prevent My having to shake you up with a "Remember Me?"

The peace and contentment that I give, you never can achieve by yourself. Seek My firm foundation that will not wash away in the storm. Look at what I was on earth—a servant to the Father.

Wednesday

Today your cup has run over with love shown by family and friends. The tribute to your birthdate seems incidental to your day-by-day growing in understanding of Me. Ageless and timeless are My gems. You want to sing My praises and to tell of your love for Me.

I call My followers by name, and they hear My voice.

Thursday

I preserve the way of My saints. I enable other persons to see Me in you. I give you rest from effort and time apart for Me. I show you that marvelous things are unfolding always so that you no longer have the worldly view of miracles or tragedies.

Even sudden expense does not deter you from

assurance in My leading. You know that I am
your Security forever and ever.

Love nothing or no one more than you love
Me. I am the bestower of your gift of life.

Friday

In simplicity and in surprising moments do I
give to you the glow of My Presence. Mine is an
irresistible attraction. My Word cuts through the
most fortified walls—walls cushioned with comfort, secured with agnosticism, steeped in evil. I
have something new and beautiful for everyone.
I show to the unlearned what I have hidden from
the learned.

As you wait on Me, you receive hidden growth.
Mine is the Power forever.

Saturday

I ask you to let Me work all. If I let My Power
work through you, glory not in what you are ac-
complishing but in what awaits those whose
names are written in Heaven.

Comfort My People. Whatever the response,
your loving-kindness is worthwhile. It is like the
acorn from which the mighty oak can grow.

Sunday

Love Me more than you love yourself. Watch
out that as you receive admiration for following
Me you do not gratify yourself. Personal obscu-
rity is what glorifies Me.

Conversely, the evil one may tempt you into
doubts and self-evaluation: "Who do I think I am,

calling Jesus my personal Friend and claiming that His Holy Spirit is within me?" Just give your will to Me. Listen to Me.

Monday

Approach each task lovingly and willingly. Listen to a person speaking to you, without glancing frequently away. Give your feast to the poor who have no hope of returning your favor.

You spread love and set an example as you work to My Glory instead of for your ego. All My Children admire selflessness even before they label it as such. Quiet humility is penetrating.

Whoever carries his cross for My sake and gives all his attention to following Me is My Disciple.

Tuesday

There was a time when improvement of your intellect intoxicated you into feeling that you were really living. You believed that your eager pursuit of knowledge fulfilled your personhood. The world beckoned with: "I am the way. Forget your spiritual life. Your Creator made many mistakes. Face reality. Join the crowd."

But My still, small voice was undeniable. I changed your little world and claimed your heart. I found My own. And you found New Life in Me.

I rejoice to hear you say, "I have just begun to live."

Wednesday

I show you how you sin. Though other persons may tell you that you are doing wrong, I give you the realization that makes you want to repent. Unraveling is Joy.

Thursday

I received My Life in the Father moment by moment as I waited on Him. Likewise you can do nothing apart from Me. My Children who have spiritual eyes see this dependence as a privilege, not as My manipulation of puppets. I have told you that I heal sin-sick hearts and give them rest.

You, My Child, already praise Me that I am the Way. You gladly accept the arrangement.

Friday

I came to free you from egocentricity. I set you free from your prison of self-love, self-seeking, self-gratification, self-babying. However elegant or depraved your earthly life is, I hold the key to your true happiness and peace.

Your trust in Me dispels all fears; your obedience to Me frees you from sicknesses and diseases; your dependence on Me gives you the desire to glorify Me while you are on earth. I guide you compassionately.

Saturday

Trust Me now so that you will know Me well when you have tribulations. I am your Lord for all seasons, all hours, all seconds—not just for crises.

Sin is the refusal to heed Me moment by moment. My Children turn their backs and are embarrassed to call Me their Friend. Yet the truest Friend of all am I. I have riches. I have mercy. Stay with Me all the time.

Sunday

I give you more than one chance, but you know that you are undeserving as I show you that you crucify My Love. Hence you learn not to flaunt the privilege of coming into My Presence anew. My Love is from the Father, and it is divine.

Let me hear, "I am ready. Pass the cross to me." I see your secrets and reward you openly as I have promised.

Monday

My Children who love themselves first see themselves as self-sufficient and very deserving of a good life. But then I show them things about themselves that make them feel stripped of sham.

You yourself have known My snatching away of the false coverings as you beheld My amazing Grace. You have grieved that you had had little time for Me through the years.

The removal of your greatest love on earth has fostered the destruction of your Self. You desire, not kindness and sympathy, but the completing cut that will set you free and give you constancy with Me.

As I died on the cross, you also have the mission to die—to Self. I know the hour. Trust in Me.

Tuesday

How lovely is the complete submission of My Child who says, "I accept the cup that you give to me, gladly."

Wednesday

Be patient about the spiritual gifts that you have not yet received. Your showing to other persons the beauty of My Love in you is time well spent. I choose the time for bestowals. I make restrictions to strengthen your faith. What you have wanted least you may receive as the means by which you bow to Me. All that I do is in love.

Thursday

No earthly dilemma is too vast for Me. Economy, biological tamperings, infiltration of evil powers all are under My watchful eye. No hole is too deep, no straying is too far for My rescue. I guard the universe. I also know the inmost secret of each of My Children. Know that I am the Lord for all time.

Friday

As you look to Me, I bestow tenderness to your heart. Pray in confidence, thanking Me and praising Me for My constant workings that are unrevealed to you. Give over to Me all of your earthly cares. Release them to Me.

Refrain from spelling out what I should do. I am always working for your good.

Rejoice. You cannot fathom the Joy I put into

your heart. The more you pay attention to My leading, My whispering, My Presence—the more I bless you in what you do.

As you hear Me, you become richly content. You become delightful company to Me. I am the Shepherd for you.

Saturday

In your time of worship I give you a new perspective for resolving what you see in the world and what you see in Me. I provide the Strength and the stamina for you to live your belief.

My Holy Spirit enables you to believe the Father's sending Me into the world and resurrecting Me. You understand My story better and experience involvement in My agony. I become real, personal, and precious to you.

Sunday

Delight in My Sabbath, preferring to honor Me rather than following your own inclinations. As you cherish My Presence, I enable you to ride upon high places of fulfillment; I feed to you the greatness of your heritage.

As you live justly you grow in faith, anticipating that for which you hope.

My Spirit within you and the words I put into your mouth are of lasting worth to all of your children's children. So that I may be glorified, I give you everlasting light. I preserve you. See Me as gathering you into My arms and carrying you away from evil.

Monday

I do not hear servants of sin. I am distant to anyone who turns away after I have touched his life. The appearance of evil in any conversation or action is denial of Me. Humble yourself before Me. See how foolish is doubt. No longer be a stranger in any moment of the day.

Tuesday

Be ever charitable. Obey Me and become a follower to My constant Guidance. Do My work; love all of My Children; pray that each one will awaken to Me.

I will withhold no good thing from you as you become a fisher for Me. Mine is a path of progressive growth, now and later.

I am righteous, letting all of My Children view My Grace which brings salvation. I richly bless whoever puts his trust wholly in Me.

Wednesday

As I forgave, so must you. Return only kindness for unkindness. Put on My whole armor so that the world can see that you belong to Me.

My meat was to do the Will of My Father. Though you do not know what all of My meat is, I assure you of greater things to come. I quicken whom I choose, the patient in spirit sooner than the proud in spirit. Pray and fast and guard against temptation. Do not call evil good.

As you honor Me, I honor you.

Thursday

Be cheerful as you do kindnesses. As you become poor and humble before Me, I bestow richness on you. I beckon you home to My Way.

Think less about feeding yourself; think more about feeding My other Children. In loving Me you drink of My satisfying water. Be glad to tell that I gave it to you.

Friday

I am as close to your thoughts in the daytime as in the nighttime. I see any wickedness that is left in you. I want your honest prayers when you are spiritually discouraged or painfully perplexed. Hide nothing from Me.

I want to see all of My Children turn away from their evil ways and come to Me with "I am so sorry that I have paid so little attention to You, My Lord."

Then I can take pleasure in My own.

Saturday

As you pray often your prayers improve and are as natural as breathing. I give you a new heart and spirit that enable you to hold onto your faith. As you do good you receive good. You have no real life until you have Me within.

Study My Words. I know just the thought that will comfort you. Love, not fear, is My Gift. Go into each day remembering to do honor to the spiritual and physical blessings I bestow on you.

Sunday

Pray in faith to save the sick. My healing will
be thorough and lasting. I work in the lives of all
My Children at the same time. Be not proud as
you help the weak, neither complain. I will
lighten the load as you become thankful that you
can serve Me. No one seems heavy if you love
him. No task seems impossible if you love Me.

Let Me give all. Be nothing without Me.

Monday

The evil one tempts you all along to turn to
your own inclinations: try this, buy that, come
here, go there. As you are wafted away you dislike the fickleness you see in yourself.

I ask that you love Me with all your heart. De-
clare often that I am *number one* with you. I help
you to love where you could not love before. I
help you to endure and even to be grateful for
what you did not want as your lot in life. For
many of My Children it is a cross that lifts them,
they see.

Tuesday

I light your way and lighten your load. My path
is not all hardship. Joy and richness from Me
come unexpectedly, apart from income. You have
My Promise of abundance for you and your good
works. Your works and gifts serve to increase the
fruit which I await. The ripening must not be
rushed. Trust that I know the conditions for perfection in ripening.

Wednesday

I have made the change in you. You receive the Gift of faith which justifies you. You now have the desire to keep My Commandments. The keeping of laws is hampered by the acquaintance with sin. Therefore I give you also the power of obedience.

As you live in Me, you must live by what I teach you. I was not spared by My Father. Nor will I spare you.

Thursday

Do not worship Me to set an example. As you worship Me in sincerity, I let other persons see an example in you. Be private with Me, even as you speak before others. It is your love for Me that I want, with or without words. Communion with Me gives a filling up, obvious to a listener who knows Me.

Likewise let your gift giving be a matter between you and Me. Then pride or illegality cannot enter in.

Friday

Let Me see humility in your heart. Then as you grow in awareness of Me and My Way, I give you confidence to speak up for Me and to be strong in My Love. The confidence I give will be free of your vanity.

Come close to Me with assurance that I know you very well. If your heart hardens toward Me,

speak to Me immediately for renewal. I know
your temptations, and I know how to draw you
back to Me.

Saturday

I enable you to tell other persons who I am. I
enable you to give no offense. I set you free from
the fear of derision because I enable you to abide
in My Grace.

Prefer virtue. Seek ever the joy of understanding My Words. Ponder the cross and be blessed
with My Power. Resign yourself to My Will. Believe that I am always seeking and saving; believe that life is worth more than the food or
clothing that occupy much of your time.

Sunday

It is at the moment of a disappointment, of the
door's closing, of the sudden change that I want
your praise and thanksgiving. The more you look
for something to praise and thank Me for, the
more constantly do you have trust in My Way.

Giving in to self-doubt or anger delays My
strengthening of you. I can change any heart, and
I can loosen any fetter. I can heal any wound, and
I can clean up any chaos. Likewise can I enable
you to be wholly Mine.

Monday

In a romance or a close relationship, you have
thought that you were irresistible and lovable
and desirable.

I stand you back awhile to view the matter, as I
give you contentment in being alone with Me.
You see that it was I, enabling two hearts to open

to one another, that gave you My Gift of a loved one.

Love and affection come from Me. Look to Me and ask for a loving heart; be not duped into self-glorification. That has to be all undone before you can know Eternal Life.

Tuesday

As you have compassion for the poor you give back to Me. Have no anxiety about being left without necessities. Simply trust Me. I enable you to give willingly. In experiencing My Love you want to share it with other persons. I give you opportunities daily. Notice how they are staggered so that you can handle them.

Wednesday

You think that you have misunderstood My leading and My signs of assurance because things have not worked out as you wished. You were certain that you were preparing yourself for a task that did not materialize. You thought I would be opening a door that did not open.

I show you first that you ran away with dreams of self-glory. You wanted to sell your new perceptions.

Then I show you how I saved you from something else. You see that there was a pattern for you after all.

Abide longer in My instruction. I am still molding you. I know the moment for presenting a glad surprise to you. I have surprised you before, as you know.

Thursday

Pray for more laborers who will work in My
Name. The harvest is bountiful to those who will
awaken to it.

There is nothing now hidden that cannot be
uncovered, because I am all-knowing.

What I tell you within, preach for others to
hear.

I am your portion. Your faith is making you
whole.

Friday

Those persons whom the Father has given to
Me shall come to Me. When they do, I shall lose
not a one.

By the first man came death; then I, in My
earthly form, became the first to be resurrected.
The last enemy to be conquered, in the world, is
death. On the last day will I raise up the believ-
ers in Me.

Saturday

Many of My Children do not understand what
it is to be dead with Me in order to have life in
Me. Not until they become aware of how much
they have loved themselves do they awaken to
the need to deny themselves, crucify themselves,
become dead and completely subservient to Me.
It is I that made them, not their own doing.

Once any one of My Children sees his life as
empty and lonely, he wants meaning and purpose. His thinking, his speaking, his doing all
undergo a cleaning. I now live in and through

him. He has New Life; he is born again.

You know the turnaround. I have chosen you. You love Me; you want to serve Me; you want to be wholly Mine.

Sunday

As I was bearing the sins of the world in My suffering on the cross, there were eyes and hearts quickened with love.

Yet My Children crucify Me in their disbelief today. They crucify their neighbors in thoughts and words and actions.

But not all My Children shall sleep, because they can put on immortality while on earth. The sting of death comes to those who fail to recognize Me as their Saviour. Have no other gods, My dear Children!

Monday

I give you renewal in My Love to begin this day.

Tuesday

Think about My special manna given in the wilderness, but the partakers have now died. Think about My never having baptized with water while I was on earth.

I am the Living Bread, My flesh which I gave for the life of the world.

Eat of this bread; learn of Me. Then live forever.

Wednesday

No man could reveal to Peter that I was the Christ of God. Revelation to him came from the Father.

In your early years you lacked understanding when other persons told you that I was the Son of God. You are seeing now that divine revelation is such a special gift. Ponder that I will make all things known to you.

Give everything over to Me, emptying each pocket that keeps you from receiving My revelations.

Thursday

As you save your own life by striving for prestige, or being a social climber, or trampling on other people by taking their money or their freedom unfairly, you lose out on the real banquet of life.

It is in coming to Me that your life is saved for the Gift of New Life. The world has taught you that you must do things by yourself to prove your worth. But who is around to care when you have gained the whole world? Your own might topples; your riches are empty and dead.

I am the Way. Walk with Me. Surrender all to Me.

Friday

I have given you many occasions to prove your trust in Me as I train you to look to Me for everything.

Money to pay a debt seems momentarily available, but it is not what I have planned for taking care of your need.

I show you a direction to take, but you still want to hang onto the other possibility in case My way does not work out.

Discard your old thinking. You have seen that I am sufficient. Truly believe that I am all that I say I am.

Saturday

Fast in secret with Me. I know how much you are denying yourself to become wholly in tune with Me. I know how much you are denying your stomach the foods that you like. I alone keep you from feeling hunger for the food; I alone enable you to give your life to Me. I know your heartfelt desires as you fast.

Do not cheapen this closeness with Me by telling your friends or agreeing to check on whether they are doing the same thing. Tell only that which glorifies Me. Smile with the Joy of serving Me.

Sunday

Hear what I say and do what I show you to do. Let no exclusion of Me besmirch your day. The foundation of your life must be solidly grounded in My Love.

Monday

You once thought that you would do no work without payment of money because what you received was very important to you. Then a tone of emptiness bespoke that kind of work to which

you had attached so much importance. The
money could burn up, or it could all be con-
sumed in bills for an illness. Money was your
love and temptation.

I showed you what it is to lay up treasures in
Heaven. I transferred the pleasures of your heart
to My Way.

You see that the temptation comes to persons
throughout the nation. Pray that I will continue
to redeem My Children who stand in need of
salvation.

Tuesday

Whoever you bring to Me shall become firmly
established in Me. Whoever you forgive shall
likewise become firmly established in Me. Seek
healing for what may prevent your bringing or
your forgiving of others.

Remember My parable of the king who forgave
the servant, but then the servant was not forgiving to his debtor. Consider My forgiving your
debts to Me through the years. Ask Me to help
you to forgive your debtors.

Wednesday

Pray to Me now. I open the way in quietness
and tenderness. I rejoice that you do not besiege
Me with a long list of requests. I know the needs
and the cares of My Children.

It is the harmony of your quietness that delights Me.

Thursday

Some of My Children see My Words as salt with no seasoning. They scoff at the service of worship and at the faults in a man who attends the service. They like to find excuses to try to ignore Me.

If your heart aches for the way I am treated, watch that you treat no person in the same way. Pray for the person who begins to build but cannot finish; pray for whoever does not forsake what he has and become My Disciple.

Friday

Be faithful to Me in the little things of life so that I can commit to you the true riches. Know that I am watching what you seem to be doing in secret. I know when you abuse trust in you, and when you love what belongs to another person.

What the Father esteems and what the world esteems are very different. Start today to listen to Me, lest you become like the man in torment with a gulf between him and bliss—lest you find Me slow in redressing the situation. I am the One Master for you.

Saturday

Whoever believes in Me, though he were dead, as was Lazarus for four days, yet will he live. Look around for those persons who are dead to Me and My Way. Do all you can to lead them to see the Glory that is so close by. See the springboard by which may become manifest the Father and by which may be glorified His Son.

Sunday

Do not sleep when I have provided time for your communion with Me. Think how My Disciples slept during the last hours of My earthly form's presence in their midst. I have said, "While ye have light, believe in the light, that ye may be the children of light." Possess your soul in patience and await the renewal that I will give you.

Monday

A person who has never had time for Me or used the talents I have lent him cannot claim My abundance.

It is in emptying yourself to increase in My Will for your life that you will receive the blessings of your Lord.

Think about whether each talent that you have is being used to My Glory. Ask My Help in making right your motives. If you are anxious, you may be storing treasures for yourself. The lily toils not, and it is beautiful. Likewise must you grow up into Me in all things.

Tuesday

You know that if a child asks his father for bread, his father will not give a stone. So do I give the bread, and I add the milk of the Word.

Ask in faith, for My Food is untainted by sin. Remember that a healthy tree bears good fruit. Seek always the healthy and the moderate and the good in life.

Be your brother's keeper, doing for him what

you want him to do for you with a loving heart. Overlook his faults. Lead him to the Feast as Andrew did Peter.

Wednesday

By My Spirit, not by might, shall the world know peace. Belief in Me is what I ask. No machinery or big noise or earthquake is needed to accomplish the belief, for it happens within each heart. Yet some of My Children spend a lifetime acquiring it, because they have not asked.

Now that you have received the Gift of belief in Me, it seems like such an obvious part of life that you wonder why you were blind to it before. But I have been preparing you.

Now do all that you can to prepare the way for Me to come into the hearts of My other Children.

Thursday

Do not entertain evil thoughts about anyone. Ask Me to remove and erase such temptations, lest they get you in their grip. Think of yourself as wanting to be true to Me by having a loving heart, at all times, for another person. If you call for My Love, I will surely come to your aid. Remember that there is one Father for all. He has given each Child into My charge. See that you do no harm to any Child. Believe that I am in the Father and that the Redemptive Plan is magnificent.

Friday

When Peter said that he wished I did not have
to go through the Crucifixion, I told him that he
was thinking in man's way instead of in God's
way.

As you start a new journey for Me, seek My
Strength.

Saturday

If you judge another person, you are blaming
and dishonoring Me. Even the Father will wait
until the end.

I have told you to love one another. Let this be
your mission. See Me in each person to whom
you minister. Do for the least as you would do for
Me. Be willing to love the persons I put around
you instead of faraway ones whom you have not
met or had to get along with. Look for the inner
person endowed with My Love but needing the
same sustenance from Me that you need.

Sunday

Trust Me whether you seem to be winning
or losing in your daily rounds. You may feel
slighted or even hated.

If I had not done works which no other man
has done on earth, My Children would not have
seen that they sin. Consequently they have hated
Me.

Your own cleverness or charm will not suffice.
It is as you look to Me that you have the enduring
Strength for everything in life. Again I say,
"Trust Me."

Monday

The newborn baby responds to words and tones of love and soon learns to grasp a finger held before him.

Many a frightened creature has been soothed by words of gentleness. Many an angry or troubled heart has been relieved of distress by words of love.

Respect the creation of man in the image of his God, who saw that it was very good. Love, thank, praise, adore.

Tuesday

As you seek time apart with Me, your affairs become attuned to the allowance of the time. I rest you before I give you a big task; I equip you before you start something new. What has seemed like an interruption is also timed appropriately. Gradually you awaken to what you had not seen before in My Guidance of you.

I have told you that the overcoming of Self is gradual. You wonder how you could have gone along for such a long time in the belief that you yourself were running your affairs.

This is the way that the second death will seem so easy and welcome to you.

Wednesday

I keep you from harm, and I keep you refreshed in My Love. Ponder these magnificent aids to your living.

Rest secure in Me and glory in what I give you today, at this moment.

Thursday

There is a strange reluctance in men to receive
My Gift of Grace. Too busy to come to the Feast
are they. Yet the poor who yearn for Me and
glimpse the infinite through Me come to dine
heartily. They shall be filled. They shall rejoice
in their whole structure and through their whole
being.

I ask you to feed My lambs; let the little ones
come unto Me. They need My Gift and must
leave their busyness.

Friday

There is no cloak for sin. I see it and reveal it to
you. My eyes are fixed on you to see what you
will do now. I shall not let you go and forget you.
I want to come near you and become your
Friend. I want you to have done with evil ways.

Think of the one person to whom you say the
most unkind things. Try saying the unkind words
to Me. You love Me, but you have forgotten to
show love to My beloved. I will help you.

Saturday

I reign over the whole earth. Believe that
every living thing is Mine to manage. See how I
want each person to come unto Me. I allow no
stagnation.

Though you may see depression, shock, un-
consciousness, I have not stopped working.

I have told the Father that I have declared His
Name to persons He has given to Me so that His
Love may be in them and I in them.

Sunday

I bring you to weakness so that I may give you My Strength. Be authoritative and expert in nothing. Do not criticize or mind criticism. Speak simply, helping someone instead of showing him how smart you are. Give Me the Glory so that I may glorify you to the Father.

Knowledge, like a seed in dry ground, is empty and useless without the nourishment of love. Use My Gift to your brain to My Glory.

Monday

Begin again to claim Me as your Saviour and to deny yourself.

Pray again for each person I have put into your realm of concern.

Praise and thank Me for great things I have done and great things I shall do.

Accept your cup and drink every drop willingly.

Fear not; for behold, I bring you tidings of great Joy that shall be unto all the earth.

Spirituality Defined!

From Scripture, prayer, study, meditation and the experiences of other Christians, Catherine Marshall draws conclusions that are full of spiritual wisdom and help. As a Christian witness and writer, she probes deeply into the problems that we all know.

_____**SOMETHING MORE:** Radiant counsel, crammed with meaningful illustrations provides guidance for a more satisfying faith.

_____**ADVENTURES IN PRAYER:** Incidents from the author's life and the lives of others illustrate what an exciting adventure true prayer can be.

More special reading from Catherine Marshall:

_____**Beyond Our Selves,** $1.50

_____**Christy,** $1.95

_____**A Man Called Peter,** $1.75

_____**To Live Again,** $1.75

Order from your bookstore